# undisordered

## by Julia Mazzucato

# DEDICATION

*To Olivia, Mr. Hallstrom, Shira*
*everyone who's won, everyone who's lost*
*everyone who's fought, and everyone who is still fighting.*

# My Story
*What happened.*

I am no iconic author - and I will never claim to be - but F. Scott Fitzgerald and I have something in common. Throughout his career, he wrote countless iterations of the same story: his own. Fitzgerald tore himself apart for the star-crossed love of his life - chasing her through the chapters of *Winter Dreams* and the glittering parties of *Gatsby,* selling his soul and making the gravest mistakes of his life just to hold her before it all slipped through his fingers. Throughout every novel he wrote and tale that he spun, Fitzgerald could never outrun his wounded, wounding, transcendent love for Zelda Sayre. The one that got away. The green beacon of light across the water, beckoning him in. His pain echoed through the pages as he wrote and rewrote the one story for which he could never possibly write an ending.

Three years ago, I nearly died from an eating disorder. Well, multiple eating disorders, to be exact; I suffered from anorexia nervosa and bulimia at the same time, while also battling suicidal ideation, anxiety, body dysmorphia, and severe depression. My eating disorder was something I had lived with for a large part of my life, lying dormant and feeding off of my insecurities, but it only took a few short months to escalate into a debilitating mental illness that nearly killed me twice and took years to recover from. I have spent the last few years of my life reclaiming everything that I lost to my disease, and even today I am still picking up the pieces and healing myself. I never stopped recovering, and I never stopped learning from the biggest mistakes that I have ever made.

It is a story I cannot run from, and one that I cannot write an ending to. I tried for years to leave my past in the shadows behind me; I tried in vain to move on and keep living. But in ignorance there lies no bliss, and no secret can live forever. Every day that I live is touched by what I went through, and not a day goes by that I don't reflect on just how much of a miracle it is that I am here today. I couldn't escape it if I tried. My greatest battle was fought within the silent chambers of my own soul. The fight for my life against mental illness destroyed my world, but gave me the chance to rebuild its foundations stronger than before. I am who I am today because I lost, I fell, I rose, and I fought.

Just as F. Scott Fitzgerald could never seem to escape Zelda Sayre, I can't escape my past. So I have decided to stop running from it.

Besides a very dear friend and one amazing teacher, I've never told anyone this story before. Mostly because I was embarrassed. For years, this was my quiet burden, my shame. But I believe that I have finally come to a such a place of peace and understanding with my story, that I can take the pain of what I went through and use it to educate. I wrote this book to urge a shift in the way we as a society see eating disorders as a mental illness, to teach about something that has played such a central role in shaping who I am today. I wrote this with the hope that I could help at least *one* person struggling with their own battle, and maybe save a life. I wrote this because the very thing that destroyed my life built in me an immeasurable strength that I hope to use to make sure than no one ever has to live through what I did. Most of all, I wrote this to share my story - one that has lived in the dark for far too long.

But before I write an entire book about this thing, I figure you should know the overview of my story. How and when it happened, its causes and effects, the way that it slowly destroyed my life from the inside out, and how I fought to recover from the worst period in my life. That sounds dark as hell, I know. And it's no lie, this was the worst time of my life with no contest. I know that nothing I experience in my future will ever come close to the pain that I felt during these months of suffering, and the years I spent picking up the pieces. My body and my mind were at civil war, and both sides lost gravely.

It's hard to trace back to the beginning of my eating disorder (I'm going to try in the next chapter, so just you wait). But I believe that the 'seed' was planted years before it finally took effect - I guess you could say I had a dormant eating disorder for quite a bit of my life. But it all started with learning how to count calories. Flipping over boxes and checking out nutrition labels, getting a basic knowledge of how many calories was in something. I did that for years without ever really doing anything with that information. I'd read the label on a jar of Trader Joe's Cookie Butter, take note of the fact that a tablespoon was about 100 calories, and then go ham on it a few minutes later and eat half the jar with a baby spoon. Those were the days of total relaxation and blissful carelessness about my diet- because I didn't *have* to care back then. I was 10 years old.

Middle school is what I like to call a steaming cesspool of juvenile insecurity and rampant toxicity. The boys are more obnoxious, the teachers more exasperated, the girls 100 times more cruel and vicious. Adolescence brought out the worst in us all, and there I was, queen of the swamp: the notoriously inflammatory Julia Mazzucato, petty to a fault, bitingly competitive, a raging gossip, a self-centered egotist. A scared little girl, hiding behind a fake personality and a fake smile. Every insecurity that the vicious combination of puberty and my disordered eating habits had bred was projected onto my peers, and one by one, every friend that I had was alienated from my side. That's not to say that the girls at my school were any better than I was. But being the competitive person that I am, I couldn't help but compare myself to them at every turn. When my skinny friend complained on the daily about being fat and needing to lose weight, I sucked in my stomach and shrank into my sweater wondering with a panic, *What does she think of me?* When the PE teacher took our height and weight each year for the FitnessGram, I listened intently in the locker rooms as the girls chatted about their stats, comparing my own and hoping - praying - that I would hold the lowest number.

Over the months, as my stress grew, so did my attention to what I was eating. My life was spiraling out of control, everyone hated me (including myself), my grades were dropping as I focused less on school and more on dieting, and the only thing I *could* control was my food. As the days dragged on, I started taking in less and less - and paying more and more attention to it. First it was 1200 calories a day. Then 1000. Then 900. Then 800. And the most dangerous part of this was that I didn't recognize that what I had fallen into was a full-blown eating disorder. For years, I had been told that an eating disorder, or anorexia in particular, is where you don't eat *anything*. But what really happens is the toxic cycle of not eating enough to sustain your body, and doing so for the sole purpose of achieving a physique that your warped perceptions of beauty and health have placed in your mind as the ideal, the *must have.* In my mind, what I was doing was not wrong. Because I was eating. I used that sentiment to lie to myself for months, convincing myself that what I had was not an eating disorder, because food, however miniscule in amount or fulfillment, was still making its way into my stomach. Perhaps that denial was what led me into the deep, dark pit, or at least was what handed me the shovel and told me to start digging it myself.

My family started to take notice, and I started to take notice of them taking notice. I'll never forget a fateful family trip that we all took to Las Vegas. This wasn't even at my lowest days of intake - I was eating out at every meal - but my behavior was noticeable enough for my grandparents and family to pick up on. I remember hearing hushed remarks of worry being passed between my grandma and my aunt, and I remember pretending I didn't hear and then bawling in the poolside bathroom alone about it. I also remember asking to use my mother's phone one day after we had eaten breakfast with my sister and grandmother in the hotel's French bistro. I entered the iPhone's passcode, and the phone immediately opened up to her messages, where she had been texting my dad. The last message read "JJ is eating," with a covertly snapped picture of my egg white omelette from the lighter fare menu. My dad's response was a terse "good."

When we got back from the trip, my parents wanted to take me to the doctor's office, saying that they were concerned I wasn't eating enough for a "growing girl." I remember being so anxious in the weeks leading up to this appointment that would change my life forever, even if I had no idea just yet. When it finally rolled around, it was a brief one-two punch: my doctor simply said she'd like to see me gain five pounds, and I'd started to cry. Looking back, that seems like nothing. It would have been so easy just to do what she'd asked and avoid what came after. But from that day, things only got worse.

I promised my parents I could gain the weight on my own, and they trusted me. I did the exact opposite of what I was supposed to do. I restricted my eating even more, without even understanding why. This was the aforementioned period where I dropped down to eating only 800-900 calories a day, pushing my body to the brink. And in the three months that passed between that first doctor's appointment and the fateful day of April 29th, 2015, I lost fifteen pounds.

If it wasn't for my mother, the strongest woman in the world, I would be dead today. She staged her own one-person intervention and forced me onto a scale on Wednesday, the 29th of April, before I left for school. When she looked down at the number and looked up at me, I lost it - hit with an anxiety attack, a panic attack, and a sobbing fit all at once. I missed school that day for the first time that year, and I still remember it as the worst day of my life. I remember everything that I ate that day. And I remember the pain like it was yesterday.

The next three months were a living hell. I felt trapped in this failing body that was my own, drowned in my depressed and disordered mind, and plagued by deep, dark suicidal thoughts that I cannot dwell on even today. I was still eating the bare minimum of what I could do under my parent's supervision. They were still forcing me to eat more and more, to try and nourish myself, but there was only so much I could eat. After every meal my stomach would bloat and feel like it would burst, because it had shrunken down and adjusted to me starving myself for so long that it could no longer handle food. One slice of pizza, and I would be clutching my stomach in pain. My intestines were failing too - digestion was one of the most painful and long processes that my body was struggling to undertake. Of course, still restraining myself and eating very little was not helping me and my weight. I still dwindled around my lowest BMI, and my parents and a panel of doctors began to force me onto weight gain shakes, those things that old people in senior homes who can't eat solid food drink all day. I hated those. I cried so much every night when my parents forced the bottles into my hands and watched me drink until it was empty. It was torture, and not just because of how scared I had become of food. It was being treated as if I was a patient, a burden, something that couldn't take care of itself. My eating disorder had robbed me of my independence, something I'd had all my life. I had never realized how much I needed that independence in order to survive.

May 22, one month post-intervention. The worst birthday of my life.

My parents stopped trusting me. I stopped trusting them. I became scared in my own home, paranoid of their every move. They were just trying to help, I tell myself now. But even looking back on the situation with a healthy mindset today, I see their faults in the situation… and their unpreparedness. The truth is, no one knew how to deal with something like this. In both sides of my family, eating was something that was expected- eating a lot was a cross cultural element that you saw it in our Italian family, in the

Hawaiian-tinged traditions of my Japanese family, and in the American culture I grew up in. You would get to someone's house and eat their food that they served you, for the sake of hospitality and being a courteous guest. Breakfast, lunch, dinner, and everything in between was a time for belonging and love to be shared, and feeding your family was the best way to show them that you loved them. It was just what you did. And it didn't make sense to them that I couldn't just *do* what I had done so easily for my entire life.

My father faced as much denial throughout my disorder as I did, and he remained in denial even after I'd accepted what I'd driven myself into. He was angry - even *livid* - because he didn't understand what my problem was. Why the hell wasn't I just *eating?* Why wouldn't I snap out of it? I remember how he would sit down across from me while I struggled to eat the food they put on the my plate, and stare at me with a look of total devastation on his face. Sometimes I'll still catch him doing that same thing, where he grabs my thin wrist - not nearly as bony as it was at my worst - and he closes his fingers around it, staring at me like he's going to cry. That look is something I'll never forget. It was like he was mourning the death of his daughter who was sitting in front of him, barely alive. And he was right to mourn her; the girl he wanted back, his carefree and happy daughter, was gone forever. Somewhere along the way, the old me died, and I would never be the same as I was before. He didn't understand, he couldn't have - but know why he acted the way that he did. He felt like a failure as a father and as a man. He couldn't keep his daughter safe. He couldn't keep her from killing herself. And that is why he still denies it to this day. When we'd go to doctor's appointments, a nurse uneducated in my situation might look at my chart and see a sharp weight drop followed by a slow increase, and ask if I had an eating disorder, to which he'd raise both eyebrows, shake his head, and say, "No, no eating disorder!" with a slight chuckle and nervous glance at me. Maybe he'll read this book and understand, finally accepting the truth that he never wanted to face. But I still love him and forgive him in every way possible, because he loves me like no one else. He loved me so much that he hurt me.

And my mother, she took a pragmatic solution to it by treating me how she'd treat treat a kid in juvie if she was a police officer. Watching me. Making my life into a strictly regimented and observed routine where she would monitor my every move and give me harsh reprimandation if I did the wrong thing. I remember one night when I wouldn't get on the scale because I knew what the number was going to be. She yelled at me until I was sitting on the bathroom floor crying, my nose bleeding from the stress, and my breath choking out of my throat in one of the worst anxiety attacks I have ever had. She loved me too. But like my father, she didn't know how to deal with this situation, because both of them came from a culture and an era where mental illness was nothing more than bad coping mechanisms and if you couldn't function properly, like the perfect little machine child, it was your family's job to conceal, conceal, *conceal*. Both ways, it was hell. The stress of my illness brought out the worst in everyone it touched.

My sister became my refuge, my safe space, and she remains it to this day. Even she didn't fully understand what I was going through. No one could. I burdened her with this role when I really shouldn't have. It was her junior year of high school, a time when she needed to be focused on her future, working hard in school, pushing herself. But I tied her down as my caretaker, my therapist, my one safety in a house where I did not feel safe and a body where I did not feel alive. And she was loyal, understanding, never hesitated to listen to me and help me through whatever anxiety attack or dark, disturbing thoughts and tendencies I was having. For that, I hate myself, for anchoring her to me when I should have let her flourish. And for that, I will also forever love her, and know that I was blessed with the best sister in the world. Without her, I would be dead.

Speaking of therapists, during these three months I cycled through four of them. And I hated all of them so much. Three of them I never visited again after the first appointment. The one therapist I stuck with for quite a bit was the best one, even though she was still a relatively terrible therapist. The thing about therapists is, you have to find one that fits with you, and that you feel comfortable with. Your therapist cannot feel like an authority figure to you, they have to feel like a confidant. Otherwise you'll achieve nothing. Four of them wasn't enough for me to find the right one. But the last one, she came the closest to being a good therapist for me.

She had a comfy couch and a gorgeous collection of designer bags, which I loved to see whenever I walked into a session. She gave me worksheets and homework to fill out, which in hindsight is not a great way to connect with a patient who's in school. As if I really needed more homework. With her, I struggled to open up and let myself be emotional in front of her. She chalked up every issue in my life - my crumbling friendships, my father's temper, my dropping grades, my crippling anxiety - to one little, oversimplified diagnosis on a sheet of paper. Looking back on it, she said a slight permutation of the exact same thing in every single meeting, and for that reason I classify her as a mediocre-at-best therapist and a waste of money. But she was the reason that I was able to acknowledge the truth: I had an disease, and I also had a choice to make. I could either recover or die. There was no third choice. That was all I had left.

Nearing the end of these three months, I was about to go on my annual summer trip to our grandparents' house in Hawaii. Travelling used to be a joy for me, a wonderful time to leave my little California suburb and explore the world. My eating disorder has changed that for me, perhaps forever. I was so scared for this trip, and not just because it was a different place where I had no idea what I would be eating from day to day and no certainty. It was because this was a family reunion, and I didn't want anyone to see me. This was my extended family, on my mom's side. Hundreds of people who hug, and laugh, and eat. I didn't want them to feel my frail, bony body when they hugged me. I didn't want them to see me not laughing with them, because I was severely depressed. I didn't want them to watch me eat my meager little rations of food that I chewed until it was flavorless mush and then swallowed with a painful gulp. I didn't want them in my life. Leading up to this trip, I was seriously considering ending it. Suicide plagued my thoughts throughout June. Thankfully I always ended these thoughts by concluding, *no, I want to live.* It would take me forever to make the same connection to end my eating disorder as well.

Before I left for the trip, I had a therapy appointment with my last psychiatrist. She listened to me cry for an hour about my fears and anxieties going into this trip, and a month alone with my mother, who I was scared of more than anything at that time. At the end of the appointment, she told me to write a "Goodbye Letter," which I later learned was something commonplace amongst eating disorder treatments. If you want to read my Goodbye Letter, it's included in my writings from Chapter 10 of this book. A Goodbye Letter is essentially a "eff you" breakup with your eating disorder. You write it down on paper, and you read it to yourself. You use it to motivate yourself to tell your eating disorder to go to hell, basically. At the time, I remember thinking that my therapist was just spewing even more crap than usual. You can't write away a mental illness, honey. But I still wrote my letter anyways, laced with words and broken promises that I wanted to believe so badly.

For lack of better words, the Hawaii trip was a trainwreck. The family reunion was four days of torture, with endless remarks on my body and infinite "*wow, you got skinny*"s. My energy was always drained, so I would constantly need to take a nap during the day. To make me feel even more basket-casey, my mom had bulk ordered my weight gain shakes and had them delivered to the resort we were staying at, so the entire staff knew that I either had a debilitating disease or was secretly an old lady. One of the worst traits of eating disorders is that you suddenly become paranoid about who is watching you eat, or who you *think* is watching you eat. I hated when people took notice of me eating my food, especially when it was my weight gain shakes or, eventually, the calorie-dense protein bars that my mom forced me onto as well because the shakes alone weren't doing anything. So I would try to eat alone, off to the side I isolated myself. It became embedded into my subconscious, and eating around other people is still is something I struggle to make myself comfortable with now. Even today, I sit in the corner of the couch with a bunch of pillows surrounding me, because I subconsciously don't want someone sitting too close and watching me eat. It all stems from this damned trip.

Leaving Hawaii, I had never felt so defeated. This vacation, in my mind, was supposed to be my release. I was going to let go. I was going to enjoy spontaneous shave ice, ice cream, delicious white chocolate macadamia cookies... just *food*. I wanted to enjoy life again. But I did not let go. I did not loosen my reins on myself. I'd order side salads at dinners. I'd obsess, restrict, keep doing the same things that I was doing. It's crazy, how your mind works under the hold of a mental illness like this. I was terrified of losing more weight, I really was. I knew I had to gain weight in order to survive. But at the same time, a small part of my mind was praying that the number wouldn't go up, stuck in a prison of its own making. I was trapped, and I just wanted everything to stop. Everything. The noise, the pain, my life. I wanted it all to end.

I got on the flight back to California feeling like nothing had changed. I was still stuck, still trapped. I felt numb, hungry, and *so* tired. When I sat down next to my mom in the plane and pulled out my notebook, the Goodbye Letter that I had written fell out of the pages. I read it to myself, my hand shaking as the words echoed through my mind. They meant nothing. I whispered a goodbye as the plane took off from the runway: *I'm leaving you here.* Then I sat back, took a breath. It was still there. You can't just let go of it. And I knew that. As I sat there, contemplating my entire life, I asked myself the question that I'd asked before but never really answered. *Do I want to live again?* And my mind overpowered that disgusting little voice in the back of my head, and said, *Yes.*

That was my turning point. I was going to put that steel discipline and willpower to use, direct it away from starving myself and use it to force myself to recover. I set a calorie goal for each day, one that would help me slowly gain back weight. Anywhere from 0.2 to 0.4 pounds a week. Like I said, small. I had 20 pounds to gain back, so this was going to take a while. But it was in my comfort zone. I would force myself to reach this calorie goal. I had to. I wanted to live. This was the solution. I don't know how I never saw it before.

That night, I ate without the intent to eat as little as possible for the first time in nearly a year. I had a long way to go, and I would fall plenty of times on the way there. But that night marked my first victory against my eating disorder, and from that point on, I was determined to live.

Like I said, I designed my recovery plan to take a while. It was what I was comfortable with, these slow increases over the weeks. The thought of gaining 20 pounds was overwhelming and made me want to quit before I started. But ¼ of a pound? I could do that. So I dragged out this recovery process to protect my mind from the weight gain and my body from further damage. It took my nearly a year to restore my weight, and even longer to restore my mental health. But the biggest hurdle was cleared 30,000 feet in the sky on that airplane. The rest was just a matter of perseverance and fighting for it. I won't go into too much detail about the recovery process now, since I'll be talking all about it throughout this book. But it was long, because that was what worked for me. There is no one-size-fits-all path to recovery, just like there is no one therapist who works for everyone and no one way to survive. Everyone has their own thing. This was what saved my life, having the opportunity to forge my own recovery that I was comfortable with. For some, inpatient treatment works. For others, Minniemaud works. I am me, and what I did saved my life.

That's not to say that it was all smooth sailing. I still had extreme reservations about food. I hated eating out, I hated eating with people, I hated challenging myself. I would still do it, though. I also had extreme distrust of my parents through all of this. I still cried, I still had frequent, crippling anxiety attacks. Recovery was a grueling, torturous process. The weekly weigh-ins were the worst part. My mom wanted me to weigh in every Saturday morning, supervised, because she didn't want me to lie to her. I didn't trust her, so it was my poor sister who had to supervise these weigh ins. She was amazing for it. She never got annoyed. She always got out of bed and came to the bathroom with me. She knew that I hated it. She held my hand. She lessened the pain. Throughout the two and a half years of weight restoration, most of it was relatively awful. But it was worlds better than those three months of hell. My hair stopped falling out. My body looked less dead. My life was coming back.

And it was all worth it. Recovery was worth it. I said earlier that you have two choices in an eating disorder: you can recover, or you can die. I chose life. I chose to rebuild myself, and I'm so much better for it. I've never told anyone my story until now, because for a long time it was shameful to me. But now I see that it is a story of vibrancy, perseverance, miraculous recovery, and making the hardest choice of my life. This is my Zelda - my inescapable truth - and I want to tell you all about it. I want to tell you how it started. I want to tell you who and what I hold responsible for it. I want to tell you how I conquered my inner demons, and hopefully help anyone who is struggling with theirs do the same. Thank you for choosing to read my story.

# Where I Trace it All Back To

*Learning to count, Las Vegas, and peanut butter in Hawaii.*

I learned a lot of things from magazines. Growing up, we had a ton of random magazines lying around the house, hundreds of issues that my mom was subscribed to but rarely read. Glamour Magazine gave me a far better sex-ed class than any school program I've ever taken and taught me of what it means to be a feminist. From Time, I learned about politics, taxes, and the fact that the world is a generally nasty place. And from the glossy pages of People Magazine, I learned pop culture. Inane gossip. And I guess you could say the origins of my eating disorder were learned there as well.

People Magazine publishes "The Body Issue" every year, which includes incredible weight loss stories of both celebrities and regular people, and shows some of the sexiest celebrity bodies of the year in the shiny paper pages of a famed tabloid. They have one section that they actually include in every single People magazine, and I've quite frankly never seen such an irresponsible and damaging column in my life. It's called *What I Eat in a Day*, and it depicts the approximate daily calorie intake of a celebrity by outlining everything she eats in a day. I can only hope that they have cancelled it by now, but I remember the first time I saw it as a little girl. I read every single word, and then re-read it. Fascinated. Enamored. Addicted.

I remember the issue that I was reading had three celebrity females in it for the *What I Eat in a Day* section-

Maria Menounos, Stacy Keibler, and Khloe Kardashian. All gorgeous, and all healthy eaters. The thing about this section is that it's straight up bull. What they do is get an outline of some meals that these women eat sometimes without actual quantities or measurements of food, information they probably collect from a representative and not the actual woman. Then they approximate the calories of a loosely defined breakfast, lunch, dinner, and one or two snacks, and make an approximated calorie count for the day. For example, it might list that Khloe eats a sweet potato, salmon, and sauteed kale for dinner, and it approximates the meal to be about 350 calories, when it could be more than that. It seems to be a helpful column, providing the reader with healthy meal options and motivation for a fit lifestyle. Intent is not the problem here. It's that they show a total calorie count, more than likely a non-factual one, and it's always *dangerously* low.

I remember that issue plainly. I had pored over that spread over and over again, looking at every single thing they ate throughout the day. Every meal was super healthy. They snacked on nuts and fruits. It looked like a lifestyle to aspire to, and aspire I did. But the approximation of the calories for Maria's day was 1007 calories. For Stacy, it was 1260. And for Khloe, it was 1487. They probably eat much more than that - I'd *hope* they eat much more than that. They're grown women, and the stupid approximations are inaccurate. But my 10 year old self didn't know that. Those numbers stuck with me. Those images stuck with me. Toned, bronzed, skinny women in bikinis, who ate a lot less than me.

I believed the article and searched for it every time a new issue of People would come to my house. It was a weekly game, searching for the What I Eat in a Day spread and ogling the meals, the calorie total, the words of a "nutritionist," who would rationalize and support these ridiculous, dangerous calorie counts and diets, calling them light, balanced, healthy, clean. And for the life of me, I can't understand how they have published an irresponsible column for so long. The majority of their readers are young, impressionable, insecure women and girls like me, who will see those numbers and those beach bodies and feel like they have to change.

For years I followed the 'Khloe' diet, trying to hit around 1400 a day. And that wasn't the worst thing I could do as a tiny middle schooler- 1400 was actually right around maintenance for me and my body, as a 4'10", 75 lb girl. Puberty hit, I grew two whole inches (wow), and I gained weight, like any normal human would. But over the months, I became more self conscious about that higher number on the scale, the fact that I was buying new jeans to replace the ones that no longer buttoned after 7th grade. I started shooting for 'Stacy'. And then 'Maria'. At the worst of my eating disorder, I was getting no more than 800 calories a day. Why? Because I was indoctrinated by a stupid column in a tabloid.

Las Vegas made me realize that I was getting criticized for my eating habits. At this time, I wasn't even tracking calories, I was just consciously seeking out lighter options. Not the worst I could do, right? My family didn't think so, and they started making comments when I'd order an egg white omelet or a kids cheese pizza. Things I'd never order now of course, because I'm a passionate vegan for animal rights reasons, but at the time I saw them as lighter foods, a smaller portion or a healthier option.

I think this is where I realized that I had to be secretive, isolated. If people were going to criticize my eating, then they should never see me eating, right? I stopped trusting my parents. I'd get uncomfortable if my grandparents would ask me what I was thinking of ordering. My grandma does this thing where she peers at everyone's food and asks why they are eating it, as a grandma does to make all her grandchildren feel included and give us that classic granny warmth. I hated that so much.

A few weeks after Vegas, we spent Christmas in Hawaii at my grandparents' house. I was a new vegetarian at the time and my mom became obsessed with me getting enough protein. I was so annoyed at her for trying to force me to eat things, and she made me buy a bunch of proteiny things at the grocery store. I later realized that she wasn't actually caring about me getting protein, she was making sure I was getting food. But she made me pick out peanut butter, string cheese, veggie burgers. I remember seeking out the lowest calorie peanut butter I could find, which turned out being difficult as all peanut butter is pretty fatty. I settled on a jar of Simply Jif, and when I looked at the label, I saw that there were 14 grams of fat in the peanut butter. And that the serving was two tablespoons. Holy hell, I'd been eating peanut butter by the spoonful all these years. In that moment I felt something I'd never felt before, and something that would consume my life as I knew it.

I felt disgusting.

Literally grimacing, I looked at the string cheese and saw that it had only 5 grams of fat, much less. This seems unimportant. But this was where I learned how to count macronutrients. When I got home, I bought fat free feta, fat free sour cream, low carb tortillas, light bread, sugar free syrup. I bought a ton of artificial, nasty crap because I was obsessed. This became a game to me, finding the lowest calorie foods. I remember this one brand that had calorie free syrups, which at the time, I thought were the greatest thing. My taste buds were totally shot and I really enjoyed things that were sickly sweet or ridiculously spicy - a characteristic side effect of starving and depriving yourself to a point of just wanting *flavor* on your tongue. I tried a drop of that syrup a while ago and I realized it was disgusting. The whole time, it was horrible, but I'd never even noticed. Because I was lying to myself the whole time, telling myself over and over again that I was okay. That I was just being healthy. That this was what I needed to do.

I think this goes to show that the seed of mental illness can be planted from the smallest moment. For me, it was reading that magazine as a ten year old little girl, lying belly-down on our shaggy carpet in the living room on a California summer day. I kept that issue of People in my desk, and I would read it and re-read it over and over, fascinated by something I couldn't quite put my finger on at the time, but that I now recognize as my own insecurity, being attacked on all fronts by these women in bikinis, boasting their five-almond snacks and 1000 calorie meal plans. American beauty standards, forced into the mind and the psyche of a ten year old girl.

And I think it also goes to show the hairline trigger that can set off that initial seed of an eating disorder in someone's mind and snowball into a mental and physical illness.  For me, it was those years of yo-yo calorie counting and dieting that led me to reading every single nutrition label on the peanut butters they sold at Times Honolulu.  And the constant, hushed whispers of my family members, murmuring, "Is she okay?" when they thought I couldn't hear it.  I grew a defensive, isolationist shield around me and my mind, which was frantically reading labels and counting numbers to conform to a beauty standard set by my ten year old self, obsessed with the photoshopped images of a beautiful, starving girl.

So, yeah.  I trace my eating disorder back to an old issue of People Magazine, a trip to Las Vegas, and a peanut butter jar in Hawaii.

# Are You Okay?

*The real experience of an eating disorder.*

I'm a firm believer that you could never possibly understand an eating disorder - the intricacies of it, the mental torture, the sheer pain - unless you lived through one yourself. I'm not sure who you are - you, my reader. I don't know who will read this book. Maybe you're curious about this mental illness and you wanted to read my story. Or you're a parent, struggling to understand what your child is going through. Maybe you're a survivor like me and you came here to read the story of someone who made it out alive. Or maybe you're battling with your eating disorder right now. Hi there. I hope you're okay.

Describing exactly what it feels like is one of the hardest things for me, because there's no possible way I can put it all into words. The easiest way for me to do it is with an allegory. So use your imagination for me.

Imagine you have a house guest that just showed up one day. You didn't even invite them to stay in your home, they just dropped in one day and decided to live there. At first it feels nice to have someone there - you were feeling a little lonely and lost before - and you feel like they are helping out around the house. Making your life a little cleaner, more orderly. You think it's a healthy relationship. Maybe you even start to love them.

You start to depend on them more, until you become inseparable. Every decision you make, you have to run it by them first for their approval. After all, you've come to believe they know and want what is best for you. Sometimes you don't listen because you are your own person and you can still have fun every now and then, but most of the time they're the ones giving you advice. They steer your life in such a direction that the things you once thought were good and fun seem foreign, even *disgusting* to you, all because they said so. And they know what is best for you, right?

Then they start telling you what to do. They take control of your own home and rule over you and your decisions. They tell you that you can't go out with your friends. They tell you to isolate yourself from your family. They teach you to not trust anyone but them. And they hurt you when you stray from their reach. They start to abuse you, tell you that you are disgusting and stupid when you deviate from their rigid set of rules. And before you know it, your house is now theirs, and you live under their thumb.

I never realized that I had an eating disorder until I heard the accounts of other people's stories - their paranoia, their triggers, their fears - and realized that they were no different from how I lived. I never acknowledged that I had an eating disorder until I was nearly dead, staring at the diagnosis sheet as I sat on the crinkly white paper covering of my doctor's examination table, the paper turning translucent as tears fell from my face onto the vellum. I didn't realize that my guest had taken over my house and took me as a prisoner until one day I went to the door and realized it was locked from the inside and I no longer held the key.

I remember when I had to stop reading the *Pretty Little Liars* series; it was all because of Hanna Marin. She was rich, beautiful, everything I wanted to be, and everything that I did not know I had already become. And the book version of Hanna struggled with bulimia nervosa and binge eating disorder. I felt a flutter of nervousness and a twinge of discomfort during Hanna's chapters when her disorder - reduced to nothing but a shameful problem that she tried to conceal from the world - was mentioned. When Hanna looked at herself in the mirror and saw nothing but her imperfections, when Hanna pinched at her midsection at the stomach fat that only she seemed to notice, when Hanna cried on the floor of the bathroom as she kneeled before the toilet... I had to put the book down every time. Or at least skip ahead a few pages until I got to a new scene. I thought I was uncomfortable because the details were too vivid, too grotesque. But I was Hanna Marin. I knelt on the floor of my bathroom, clutching the sides of the cold porcelain toilet as I choked on my own breath. I poked and prodded and pinched at my abdomen, gathering up the warm skin between my fingers and wishing that I had a knife to cut it all off. I looked at my gaunt body in the mirror and saw someone that was never good enough. I couldn't read Hanna Marin's story because somewhere along the way it had become my own.

A few weeks into recovery I had a night where I was struggling, teetering on the verge of a vicious relapse. That night, to stave off the urge to go hungry once more, to keep myself from self-harm, I decided to read the stories of survivors. And I was stunned speechless with the fact that despite the intricacies, the complications, the sheer circumstances of my eating disorder and how it had manifested itself in me, the stories of these women and men were just like mine. They felt the same way when they looked in the mirror. They feared the same things that made their hearts pound in their chests and their palms sweat.

They cried just like me. They were prisoners in their bodies just like me. And that voice in their head - the one that had deceived them and screwed them and nearly killed them - was my voice. These stories resonated in my soul because they were *me:* me with a different name, a different age, a difference gender identity, a different race. Every red flag they warned of, every sign they recounted, every part of their stories captured my reality. In my fellow sufferers-turned-survivors, I not only found comfort and community in people who knew my experience and understood what I was feeling, but I realized that had I read their stories sooner, I could have known that I had an eating disorder. Where there's smoke, there's fire. And I was blind until my fellow survivors told me where to look.

So whoever you are, my reader, I want to ask you a seemingly simple question that you might not know the answer to, because I didn't know that I was sick until it was all too late. Are you okay?

*I look in the mirror and I hate what I see. I pinch at my stomach, grabbing at the loose skin around my waist and my hips, sucking in my midsection until my ribs poke from my skin.*

*I think about food all the time, all day long. I live it, I breathe it, I never let myself enjoy it. I spend my hours thinking of what I'm going to eat, or more accurately, what I'm not going to eat.*

*I'm hungry all the time. My stomach growls and aches and I notice. It becomes a game. How long can I go on like this? The sooner in the day my stomach starts to churn, feeling empty and sore, the better. When my stomach starts to growl in second period instead of fourth like the day*

29

*before, I take a sick pride in it. Hunger becomes a drug, and I'm addicted to it. When I don't eat I feel superior to everyone around me.*

*I can't eat in front of people. When I'm with them I feel their eyes on me, watching me eat. My mind keeps telling me they're judging me. And I'm hyper-aware of what everyone around me is eating too. When we're eating together and someone is having less than me, the voices in my head scream at me incessantly. What a fatass. What a pig. I have to be the purest, the cleanest, the skinniest, the best. So I isolate myself and hide my food away. The only time I feel comfort is when I'm eating alone.*

*I can't go out anymore because of this. So I begin to make up excuses - little lies that snowball into big lies that will keep me out of social engagements - because the world is judging me. I invent allergies, I avoid people, I avoid my friends and family, and I disengage from my life because I don't want them watching me. A family dinner, a social event, any meal cooked by someone other than me sends a wave of sheer panic through my body as I fear the loss of the "control" I've cultivated.*

*I can't stand their questions and their comments and their prying into my life. How they all suddenly become doctors when they see me. "Is that all you're eating?" "You're ordering that?" "Oh, good job, you ate!" "You look skinnier." "Are you healthy?" They prod and poke and touch and try to change me and I can't let them. I can't let them ruin me. So I push them away, do everything in my power to alienate them. If they can't leave me alone, I don't need them anyways.*

*I watch the number on the scale obsessively. At first it's euphoric, watching the number drop... until I realize what I'm doing. When it dips below what I'd had in mind and keeps going, I panic. I didn't plan to go this far. I didn't want to lose this much, I was just trying to be healthy. I was just trying to be beautiful. But I can't stop. And the number keeps going down, and I can't do anything to control it, because every time I go to eat I can't break out of that pattern. I freeze, I'm petrified, and I can't do it. I can't eat like I used to. The old me is dead. I'm too far in.*

*There's a voice in my head telling me that I need to feel thin. People are staring. I push out my collarbones, I suck in my abdomen. I watch as my cheekbones hollow and my jawline narrows and my eye sockets become gaunt. I brush my hair and watch chunks breaking off, losing strands in the bristles of the brush each time. I find myself wrapping my fingers around my wrist to make sure they still touch - at a certain point I can even touch my thumb to the first knuckle of my middle finger. My stomach is my least favorite part of my body, so I'm constantly trying to cover it, crossing my arms over my belly button and curling my body inwards, trying desperately to shrink myself. I am so conscious of my midsection that I squirm uncontrollably in jeans, unbearably aware of the waistband and the bulge of stomach that becomes all I can see. You'll never catch me in shorts, I can't handle the way that my thighs balloon out when I sit down and press together. I watch with a satisfaction that scares even me as my shoulder blades start to poke out and my spinal cord becomes more and more visible. I want to hide my body away under baggy clothes, but at the same time, I cinch my waist and parade my skinniness like a sick obsession.*

*I'm obsessed with the bodies of others. I can't help but be painfully aware of the physiques of the people I'm around. If I could just look that good in a bikini. If I had her long, lithe thighs, or her fatless abs. Maybe if I had her high, prominent cheekbones. Her delicate wrists. Her gapped thighs and slim calves. Maybe then I'd be happy. But I'm never happy, because I can't stop looking around and thinking to myself, I've made myself thinner than her. Why aren't I happy? Isn't thin good? Isn't thin safe? Isn't thin what I wanted?*

*But I can't stop. They're telling me to stop. They're telling me they're worried and they want what's best for me. But how could they possibly know what's best for me? They want to ruin me. Ruin my health and my body... everything I've worked for. And I can't let that happen. So I run away and retreat even further and I keep going even though I don't want this. I don't want to keep going but I'm not in control of the car; the wheel is spinning as I crash and burn and ricochet. I'm so tired, so dizzy, so lost. I want to stop, I want to be better. But I can't do it, I have a different kind of better, I have to be superior. I want to be happy, and this has made me happy before. If I keep going, I can find that euphoric high again. And so I listen to that voice in my head whispering, "Destroy Yourself." I do it, and I do it willingly, because I don't know who I am anymore.*

*I'm so hungry, but I can't eat.*

If this sounds like you, you're not okay.

# Eating Disorders, Mental Illness, and the Psychology of Society

*A tale of denial, stigma, lies, and acceptance.*

Eight million is a pretty big number to ignore, yet somehow society never fails to amaze me with how easily rears its head from the deeply important things that it deems unsightly and ugly. It is *ugly* that seven million women and one million men suffer from eating disorders in America, which just happens to be one of the most mentally ill nations in the world. It is ugly, so society collectively agrees to sweep it under the rug and go about like nothing is happening.

Eating disorders bear the highest mortality rate out of any mental illnesses, yet by many Americans, they are not even seen as mental illnesses. And the most dangerous fact of all is that the majority of eating disorders go undiagnosed, untreated, and unacknowledged.

Because the only thing more disgusting to Americans than mental illness is talking about mental illness.

Fact: the culture and societal expectations we hold today (both in Western and non-Western culture) actively breeds and fosters eating disorders. In fact, our society does this on a scale so large that it has become more than normal; it's a way of life. It starts from childhood, as we condition our children to fear the number on the scale. Four out of five children are afraid of being fat. And we're still surprised that our young generations are growing up with soaring rates of mental illness and disorders. Make no mistake; nothing has changed except the way that we diagnose today. Fifty years ago, the prevailing culture of fat shaming and eating disorders was still there, it just went even more unacknowledged. ED culture has proliferated deeply into our society, warping the minds of children who know nothing more than what they are told every day. All hatred is learned, and if you teach a child to hate *themselves*, you create a cycle that never ends. The virtues of kindness and innocence are shattered as we teach our kids that the worst thing they can be in this world is not rude, not cruel, but fat.

One of the most dangerous mentalities that needs to be broken down is people's idea of what an eating disorder is in the first place. There is no weight requirement; any person you see on the street could be suffering from a life threatening disorder. The archetype of a sufferer of anorexia or bulimia is the rail thin, translucent skinned, bony skeleton, a walking corpse, while the image of someone suffering from binge eating disorder (BED) is always overweight. I just happened to fit the prototype body of my eating disorder - dangerously underweight - but if every person suffering from anorexia looked like me, you would see a lot more deathly skinny women and men everywhere you went. Because one in 200 women suffer from anorexia, and as many as one in five people will suffer from some type of eating disorder at some time in their life. If everyone fit the stereotypical body type of an eating disorder sufferer, you would see it in the people you know. You'd see the demons in their life, hidden behind what they choose to project to the world. Fat or thin, 70 pounds or 300 - eating disorders have no body type.

There is no specific socioeconomic status either; just because someone has grown up with a nice house, loving parents, and money to live comfortably doesn't mean that they cannot have an eating disorder, or any mental illness at that. I grew up in a two story suburban home with non-divorced parents, a good education, fancy clothes, food always in the pantry, and an upper-middle class life. I live a life of privilege that I take for granted every single day. At the worst of my depression and the depths of my eating disorder, I was plagued with constant guilt - turmoil caused not just by my struggle with food, but the underlying thoughts that told me I had no right to feel the way I was feeling. I'm a rich, half-white, educated girl in a prestigious community with every opportunity afforded to me. Who am I to be depressed? What right do I have to struggle with food when there are people starving across the world?

Whether you are rich or poor, your eating disorder does not make you selfish. Your struggle with mental illness should not be invalidated based on the amount of money you have. Because an eating disorder does not care about your situation in life - if you have nothing to lose or everything to lose, an eating disorder will not hesitate to take and take and take.

Eating disorders have no color; they are prevalent amongst *all* racial communities. While it is popularly assumed that eating disorders are most common amongst white individuals in Western countries, the most alarming increase rate of eating disorders is currently in East Asian countries such as Japan, China, Taiwan, Hong Kong, South Korea, and Singapore. There are countries where ED culture is embedded in the expectations of society. Here in the

United States, we have Victoria's Secret models advertising "The Perfect Body," which has always been supermodel-skinny. We have the diet culture bombarding us with specific vocabulary to shape our relationships with food. *Cheat day,* implying that indulging in food we enjoy and crave is a mistake that breaks the prescribed rules. *Cleanse,* telling us that we need to starve ourselves to make our bodies pure. *Guilt-free,* teaching us that the consumption of unhealthy foods should bring us guilt when in reality, a healthy relationship with food would render all foods free of guilt for simply feeding ourselves. We're indoctrinated with "low-carb" this and "keto" that and "juice cleanse" and "beach body" and "flat tummy." We warp our bodies with plastic surgery and starve ourselves on fad diets and strive for the perfect body, the American dream. In Asia, eating disorders are on the rise. This is partly because of the increased exposure to Western culture. Japan's post-war economic miracle has opened the country up to heavy Western influences on its already distinctive culture, and has marked a tangible uptick in recorded eating disorders in the nation. However, the embedded Confucian cultural values shared amongst most East Asian countries such as China, dating far back into ancient history, are also a major cause of the rising prevalence of eating disorders. Confucianism emphasizes social harmony and the roles between individuals in society, enforcing a patriarchal society that expects women to be submissive and docile. This expectation of obedience goes hand in hand with the image of the perfect Confucian woman: small, thin, light-skinned and quiet. The beauty standards of East Asia are shaped around this image and in pop culture, fat-shaming is rampant and bitingly cruel.

Eating disorders are also increasingly present in black communities, Indian communities, LatinX communities, and more. The problem is growing, and it has no color or race.

Finally, eating disorders have no gender. It's true that "traditional" examples of eating disorders like anorexia are most commonly observed amongst women, but an insidious ED culture has hovered around toxic masculinity and society's expectations from men for a long time now. Many males have an unhealthy relationship with food, seeing it as something that must be burned off in the gym or converted into muscle. One anecdote I always call to mind is an experience I had at the finish line of a five kilometer race to benefit charity that takes place every year in my town. I was sitting outside of a Starbucks after I finished the run, desperately trying to hold back vomit and bring my heart rate back down, when I saw two young boys from my high school emerging from the Starbucks, race medals draped around their necks. One of them was sipping a Frappuccino absentmindedly when his friend remarked, "You realize you're just drinking back all the calories we just burned with that thing? So there was literally no point to running that race." I watched as the boy's eyes widened just the tiniest amount; clearly the thought hadn't even crossed his mind, and here he was with his friend telling him that what he was doing was wrong. The boy forced out a laugh, breathed out, "Yeah, I guess," and lowered the drink from his lips, his face turning even redder as shame mixed with his already flushed complexion from the run. I died a little inside as I watched the boy toss the venti Frappuccino - which was practically full and had probably the guy cost six dollars - right into the trash can. When it landed in the bin, his friend gave the slightest nod (an unconscious little show of body language) and they were on their way.

With men, the culture isn't overtly obvious, but it is there nonetheless, proliferating every day through the toxic gender roles society has prescribed for men. We teach boys to hide away their emotions, to never cry, to "man up." They have to be aggressive and conventionally attractive to be the alpha male, to have a chance under the brutal social microscope. We beat them into insensitivity, telling them over and over again not to feel, and in the process we teach them to fear their own emotions. While it's true that women have higher rates of eating disorders and are perhaps more susceptible to mental illnesses in general, a staggeringly large proportion of men never report their mental illnesses, staying silent at risk of appearing weak. Society may encourage eating disorders in women, but it forces silence in men.

And elsewhere on the gender spectrum, eating disorders are abundantly present. Many trans individuals, including people who identify as non-binary, queer, or otherwise non-conforming, often suffer from one or more mental illnesses such as depression or anxiety, typically caused from their situation in life and the ostracism they face from both society and their family. Statistics show that having a mental illness such as depression or anxiety makes you even more at risk of developing an eating disorder, and these individuals, susceptible enough from facing either bigotry from the people who are supposed to protect them, turmoil and stagnation over their conflicts with their gender identity, or both, often fall prey to eating disorders and self-harm in their most vulnerable states.

It's this dangerous stigma - this ridiculous archetype of what an eating disorder is or is not - that is precisely why people are still dying today, and society is no closer to finding a cure. We have no remedy because no one cares. We make jokes about eating disorders on TV and broadcast it to our kids on Disney Channel. We make light of eating disorders everyday, joking "Guess I'm not eating tomorrow!" after a large meal and "I'm going on such a binge!" after eating two donuts at a staff meeting. We've been lied to all our lives, either telling our children nothing about eating disorders or painting a romanticized picture of an emaciated white girl, starving herself for nothing more than vanity. And I was the girl believing all those lies. I listened to my family criticise the bodies of celebrities on the red carpet while we watched the Oscars, remarking, "She looks anorexic!" and "That's not a real woman!" Their words stuck with me as I read about bulimia in a book I got in fifth grade while learning about puberty, and I thought to myself, *How could anyone be so foolish?* I lied to myself as I fell into my own eating disorder, telling myself that I wasn't fitting every single element of the stereotype, so I must be perfectly healthy. And during recovery, I listened as classmates, even close friends at school cracked jokes using the very disorder I struggled with as the punchline. The thing is, you never know what anyone is going through. All you see is what they project to the world. So they didn't know that they were making jokes about throwing up when I had struggled through four month without a bulimic purge. They didn't know what they were laughing about anorexia while standing next to a girl who had nearly died from it. They threw around suicide jokes like nothing while I listened and tried not to call back old memories of the day that I nearly killed myself.

But that's America - that's the world. As long as thinness holds a social value, eating disorders will continue to grow and spread in the world. And the only way we can stop it is to dismantle the system altogether. Reject the archetype of the ideal man and woman; let boys have emotion and vulnerability, teach girls that they should not have to make themselves physically and figuratively small. Dismantle the toxic diet culture that places burden upon food, prescribes the good and the bad, and warps our relationship with the very thing that keeps us alive. Destroy the idea that eating disorders come with a weight requirement. Educate and define to society what an eating disorder is, because understanding the problem is the most important step to finding a solution. Lift the societal stigma from eating disorders and mental illness and fight to validate the experiences and struggles of their victims. Maybe stop running those SkinnyTea and Spanx ads on Instagram.

If we want a chance at finding a cure, the first step is to pull our heads out of the sand and admit that we've created a problem.

# Dead, Dying, and Always Crying

*So this is where I thought it was ending.*

My intervention came on an overcast spring morning of April 29th, a month before I turned fourteen. It was a Wednesday - late start for school, which meant that I would get to sleep in for an extra thirty minutes or so… but not today. My mom woke me up with a gentle shake of my arm, and I opened my eyes. She was gripping my bony shoulder in her hand, staring at it with a look on her face that I thought was deep contemplation at the time, but I now know what it was. Complete, utter pain. Etched across my mother's face, deep in her eyes and she moved her gaze from my hollow shoulder to my confused face. She said to me, in a quiet, commanding, and utterly terrifying voice, "Come with me to the bathroom and get on the scale."

Had my dad and my sister not been asleep a few rooms over, I would have screamed.

Instead, I started to sob uncontrollably, smashing my face down into my pink floral pillowcase and twisting myself into my blankets. I wouldn't let her take me out of my bed. I couldn't. What she didn't know was that I'd been faking my progress for the past few weeks, telling her that my weight had been improving. My poor mother, who had woken up at 5:30 in the morning just to do this, had to pry the blankets off of me and physically pull me out of my bed. I cried even louder, and at this point I didn't even care that my family was still asleep in the rooms next to mine. I sobbed in the dark hallway, leaning on my mother as she half-walked, half-carried me to the bathroom. There was our little glass scale, sitting on the floor. A device that would be the epicenter of the worst months of my life. She told me to get my crap together and step on it. I was hyperventilating, tears streaming down my face, and I knew that if I stepped onto that scale, my lies would be exposed and my facade would all come crumbling down.

I stepped onto the scale.

With that number, that small, deadly number, I sank down to the bathroom floor and laid there, shaking with sobs. My entire dying body quaked while I choked on my own breath, the salty water from my puffy red eyes getting in my mouth, my nose, my ears. My mom, standing above me, stared down in shock, eventually crouching down and helping me to my feet as my breathing turned from guttural chokes into quiet gasping hiccups. She stared at her mess of a daughter, bewildered by what I had done. And then she said seven words I will never forget. "Don't you ever lie to me again." She left the room, called my dad, and then called a bunch of doctors.

An hour later I sat downstairs at our kitchen table, across from my father. I couldn't even look at him, because he was staring at me with so much heartbreak in his eyes. He didn't understand. He couldn't have. I can barely remember what he said to me anymore, it's so faded into the back of my memories, my brain cells warped from months of starvation. I know why he acted the way he did. He couldn't keep his daughter safe. He couldn't keep her from killing herself. That's why he still denies it to this day. But those eyes, I'll never forget how he looked at me, how he *still* looks at me sometimes. Like I was his biggest failure.

I remember everything I ate that day like it was yesterday, because that was the day that they cooked my food. First came the breakfast of my nightmares: a piece of multigrain toast with peanut butter, a cup of chocolate cereal, and a bowl of full fat yogurt. I sat there at the table sobbing quietly, not touching my breakfast, while I watched my dad making the lunch they were going to force me to bring to school. It was a grilled cheese sandwich on whole wheat bread, with two slices of swiss cheese, avocado, and a crapton of butter. At school, I actually did eat a bit of the sandwich, but not before I pulled off the pieces of bread that had come into contact with butter and threw them in the quad trash can. When I got home, my mom was already there, and she cooked my dinner that night. It was the first time anyone other than myself had cooked me dinner at home in nearly two years. 6 cheese raviolis coated in marinara and dusted with parmesan, and two scrambled eggs with the yolks in there (despite my protests). And she actually sat down and watched me eat on the couch. I ate four of the ravioli, and had a bite of the scrambled eggs. She seemed satisfied enough, and got up to make her own dinner to come join me on the couch. And then I did something truly disgusting.

My eating disorder made me do some repugnant things, whether it was puking into a ziploc bag, binging on a protein bar while sitting on the toilet pissing, or hiding uneaten food under seat cushions to get rid of later, even though I would sometimes forget to dispose of it and I'd find it a week later. Even some morally nasty things, like throwing away food that could have gone to one of the

43

various third world countries where people go hungry every day. This thing that I did was a combination of all the worst things I could do.

I took the remaining ravioli and the scrambled eggs and I stuffed them into the waistband of my yoga pants. The food was right up against my stomach's skin, wet and noticeable and totally forming a little bulge in my waistband, but covered up by the sweater I was wearing. After my mom finally let me go, I went upstairs to the bathroom and pulled the two remaining ravioli and scrambled eggs out of the yoga pants. Then I flushed them down the toilet to get rid of evidence. I would continue to do this at school with the pasta lunches from my dad, and with various other dinners.

I thought I had made it through that day all clear- I'd still managed to consume less than 1000 calories somehow, and while that was higher than I'd had in months, I was still satisfied at the way I had evaded everything. And then my dad returned from Ralph's Grocery, with a huge bag. My mom glanced over, then stared at me and without looking back at him, she said, "Bring them over." He hauled the plastic bag over to the table and out of it he pulled a 12 pack of Ensure Plus shakes. I broke down sobbing on the couch.

Ensure, if you don't already know what it is, are those weight gain shakes you feed your dying grandpa in the senior home. It's for people who need compact calories to keep their weight up- the ones my dad had brought home pushed on 360 calories per tiny 8 oz bottle. They were comprised of chemicals, sugar, and fat basically, mixed up into one powdery-tasting chocolate concoction in a demeaning little bottle. My worst nightmare. These were for geriatric patients, old folks who were withering away. So maybe you see why I threw such a fit.

My mom pulled out a bottle from the 12 pack, twisted off the little metal and plastic cap, and handed me the bottle, saying in a cold, emotionless voice, "Drink it." I was wheezing and coughing, tears blocking up my eyes, snot dripping from my nostrils, my throat closing up and blocking my airway as I struggled to inhale. *No. NO NO NO NO.* I don't know if I was saying it out loud or screaming it in my head, but I remember shaking my head so vigorously that I ended up with a pounding headache. But then I looked up at my father, and I saw that he was crying too. Tears, streaming down his face as he tried to turn away so that I couldn't see him. My mom sat there, visibly frustrated at the fact that her teenage daughter was having a literal temper tantrum in her living room. I heard my dad softly say, "Please, Julia." It was the quietest, most heartbroken thing I have ever heard in my life. So I took the bottle from where it sat on the coffee table and I took a tiny sip. It was sickly sweet, and the fat coated my tongue, the chocolate-powder residue lingering as an aftertaste as I swallowed the milky liquid. Hating myself and what I was about to do, I drank the shake for him, and he was visibly relieved. Emptying the bottle, I placed it on the table and that was that. I was done for the night. I could go upstairs and sleep.

But I didn't. I locked myself in our upstairs bathroom, the one me, my sister, and my mom all share. It has a rainbow painted on the wall in the little separate room with the toilet. I stared at the rainbow as I got down on my knees in front of the short white throne, pulling my thinning hair back behind my head. I hesitated for a second, my eyes glazing over as I struggled to come to terms with what this would mean - what this would make me. Could I handle being *that* girl? The one that I never wanted to be… the bulimic anorexic girl? *Yes.* I stopped hesitating and I jammed three fingers down my throat.

It didn't work at first like it does in the books and the movies, and I tried for 10 minutes, repeatedly gagging on my hand until I couldn't breathe anymore. I could still taste the chocolate shake on my tongue, and I nearly felt it in my esophagus. This was my first time trying to throw up, and in about a week, I would finally figure out how to do it so that it would actually work. I actually rarely purged during recovery - some people with severe bulimia do it multiple times a day, I did it maybe ten times in total - it was too painful in my throat and I hated myself every time. I would, however, attempt it almost every day, sticking my fingers in my throat as I knelt over the toilet. I wasn't good at it, and it rarely ever worked, but when it did, it was messy - my fingers burned with hydrochloric acid, my lips dried out, my throat felt tight and scratchy like I hadn't had a drink in days. But this time, nothing came up, so eventually I sank to the floor sobbing, staring up at the rainbow on the wall until I finally gathered the strength to pull myself up and walk to my bed.

I got up and unlocked the bathroom door, walking out into the hallway. I ran straight into my sister, tears still streaming down my face. They hadn't stopped since dinner. My strong, powerful, unvanquishable older sister looked so small, so defeated, so *scared.* She pulled me in like it was the last time she would ever see me. Maybe she thought I was going to die the next day. I certainly could have. But as she squeezed my frail, bony body, and I somehow gathered the breath to whisper, "I'm okay. I'm gonna be fine." It was all a lie at the time. But she started crying too, and eventually let me go. I cried myself to sleep that night. It was the worst day of my life, and it always will be.

The next day was a doctor's appointment, directly after school. I love my doctor now, but she wasn't available that day, so it was a new doctor that I'd never seen before, my dad sitting there in the corner, looking like he was trying not to cry, and my mom in her work clothes, looking emotionless and professional - this was business as usual. The doctor came in and talked to them about my condition. I didn't hear a word. In that moment the world blurred and ebbed like it does in the movies and I felt like I was underwater, drowning. The whole time, tears were gathering in my eyes for no reason at all. I would find myself doing this often throughout my depression - staring off into the distance, crying at nothing.

Then the doctor shooed my parents from the room and asked to talk to me.

Alone.

I started to hyperventilate. She told me there was no reason for that. Sitting down next on the paper-covered examination bed, in the room with the fire trucks painted on the wall, she put her hand on my shoulder and asked me what was going through my mind. I broke down right there.

"I didn't want this to happen. I didn't mean for this to happen."

I was telling the truth, for once. The words came out of me as difficultly as my vomit did, through chokes and coughs and frantic inhales. I told her what I was really feeling. Lost, stupid, and like this was all a bad dream.

I wanted it to end.

She wanted me to see a therapist.

The next few months were all a blur. This year in my psychology class I learned that people will deliberately block out traumatic experiences, expelling them from your brain and literally not being about to remember them anymore. Maybe that's why I barely remember it - like a foggy dream that was so vivid while you were asleep, but a few minutes after waking, you can't quite remember what really happened. But I also learned that the brain, when starved of glucose and adenosine triphosphate, will literally not be able to process your memories, because it's diverting its power to literally keeping you alive. From what I remember, it's no wonder that I don't remember anything. Between the trauma, the tears, the *hunger,* it was a living hell.

The months dragged on, and I lived this nightmare alone. I told no one at school. It probably wouldn't have been too hard to guess at that point- I look back every now and then at pictures of me, and I'm shocked with how dead I looked. Back then, I thought I looked fine. The thinness didn't show up in mirrors.

I graduated middle school, faking grins and laughs at promotion dance and the graduation ceremony. And summer before high school started. My sister was shipped off to England to study abroad at Oxford, and just like that my safe spaces, away from my home and my parents, were gone.

It was time to go to Hawaii for a family reunion with my mom. We left in late June, first staying in Honolulu, Hawaii. I snuck a full bottle of pain pills in my bag, and I don't think I even had a reason for it as I was packing. But I put it in there, just in case. And off we went to my grandparent's house. Most of this trip, just like most of this period in my life, remains a blur in my mind, save the few vivid moments that changed my life forever. I barely remember Honolulu, but I can imagine it included the following: crying in my room, dodging fear foods like the plague, protesting my mom's efforts to get me to eat something, hiding from family. And so much crying. I tried to conceal it from my family, and most of all, my baby cousin. I didn't want him to see me like this. I didn't want any of them to see me like this.

Soon enough we left Honolulu and flew to Kona for that family reunion I had been dreading. Like I said, a Hawaiian-Japanese family revolves around two things: ono and ohana. Food and community. Two things I avoided at all costs.

We stayed in a condo with my grandparents, my cousins, and my aunt and uncle. I immediately volunteered myself for the loft bedroom, isolated in a level high above the rest of the condo. There I would spend most of the reunion. The combination of humidity, activity, and starvation was starting to take its toll, and I was sleeping for hours during the middle of the day. Just walking out to the pool and being in the sun for an hour would exhaust me. And when I'd stand up too quickly, the world would go black. My head would pound as I staggered around until the dizzy feeling faded. I could barely walk across the beach at this point without everything hurting.

This is where I started to get scared. Scared out of my mind that one day I would fall asleep and never wake up. At that point, it could have happened.

Finally we left Kona for the last leg of our trip: a visit to a beautiful beachside resort on the Big Island. Just me, my mom, and my grandmother. It really was heavenly. The air smelled clean and fresh, the beach was *right there*, there was a freshwater lagoon, waterslides, hot tubs, literal birds chirping outside my windows. If I believed in heaven, I would say it looked something like the Waikaloa. We were only there for four days. Like everything else, it was a blur, oscillating between intense waves of emotion and cold numbness. But there is one memory I could never forget. My suicide attempt.

July 2015, Waikaloa Resort. This picture was taken 5 hours before my attempted suicide. I was at my lowest weight.

It was a warm, humid night: our last one at the resort before my mom and I flew back home. My grandma wanted to treat us to a dinner at the fancy restaurant on the grounds, so we got decked up in our nice clothes. My mom and grandma had ordered appetizers to start, and I sat there, drinking water glass after water glass, my fingers shaking as I looked over the menu in a panic. There was nothing. Nothing that I deemed acceptable to order. Except a little garden salad, made with local greens and tomatoes and light lemon vinaigrette. But that wouldn't be acceptable to my mom. So my mind raced, my palms sweated, and I lost my mind over a salad. I panicked. When the waiter asked for my order, I said, nearly crying, "The salad, please." The waiter was startled by my shaking voice, but jotted it down and quickly averted his gaze. I barely glanced over at my mom, and looked down at my trembling hands when I saw the expression on her face. Hurt.

The salad came. I picked at it gingerly, painfully aware of my mother's eyes watching me as I ate every last bite in the small bowl. I crunched for what seemed like hours on hearts of palm, waiting for everyone else to finish their food. Everyone in the restaurant was looking at me, I just knew it. They had to be watching me eat, whispering to each other, "Look at that anorexic girl. Look at the way she pokes and prods at her little salad. She's going to die."

After dinner, my mom turned to me. All she had to say to me were two words.

"You promised."

And I broke down sobbing in the middle of the bougie restaurant with the $16 side salad. The waiter glanced my way and I got up, running for the restroom and locking myself in the big stall at the end. Emotions flooded me, clear and vivid in my mind as if it were yesterday. I repeated in my mind over and over again. *You failed. You did this. You are going to die. You failed. You did this. You are going to DIE.*

We went back to the room, small talking as we walked across the beautiful resort. My mom and grandmother dropped me off in the room and went off to the hotel gift shop to buy postcards and bath salts. I was planning on showering and going straight to bed. I was so *tired.* But something made me walk over in my fancy too-large dress and my heels to the balcony. It was 7:00, and the sky was golden as the sun began to set. The waves were lapping at the white sandy shores and the hibiscus and birds of paradise bloomed in the gardens below me. If I was going to die, this would be the place.

I went inside, grabbed a water bottle, and I unzipped my suitcase, pulling out the full bottle of pills and stopping to hesitate for just a second. I had a decision to make: was I really going to do this? *Yes.* I popped one into my mouth. Two more. I swallowed 23 pills. I planned to do the whole bottle of 120. It would be fast and painless, the most considerate and tidy way to go out. No blood, no way that I could botch it. I didn't want to die a slow and painful death in an inpatient hospital, a feeding tube jammed down my throat as my organs failed one by one, my heart slowing to a stop. I didn't want to die of an eating disorder, how pitiful would that be? I didn't want to die like that. I didn't want...

I didn't want to die.

It seems a cruel twist of irony that bulimia is what saved my life. But as I sat there on the balcony chair with my water bottle and the open bottle of pills there, I had never felt more stupid in my life. I didn't want my mom to come back and find my body. I didn't want my sister to give my eulogy. I didn't want my eating disorder to win. I didn't want to die. So I ran to the bathroom faster that I've ever moved in my life. It's a wonder that my frail legs could carry me at the speed of Usain Bolt, but I was knelt on the bathroom tiles in a split second, clutching the sides of the toilet bowl. This time I didn't even have to stick in my fingers, the disgust was making me sick enough as I emptied the contents of my stomach - pills, salad, protein bar and all into the toilet. If I had waited too long and the pills had dissolved, I might have been gone. Thank god I hadn't gotten further into the bottle. And I didn't want to take any chances, so I yanked on my uvula (that dangly thing in the back of your throat) until my throat burned with acid and I was sure that my stomach was depleted. I flushed it all away, wiped up the evidence, took a swig of water to calm my flaming throat. And I knew that my mom and grandma were coming, so I rushed out to the balcony and cleaned up the pill bottle, tucking it away in my suitcase. When I got home I would place it back into the medicine cabinet from whence it came like nothing ever happened.

I sat there on the balcony in the armchair, watching the waves go in and out, and I decided that no one needed to know. I wouldn't tell my mom. I wouldn't tell my sister, or my doctor, or my therapist. I never told anyone. This was my secret. This was my shame. I now knew that death wasn't the answer, and in a way, this was my first step to recovery, and my first step to safety.

I grabbed a protein bar to refill my stomach a little bit and sat there out on the balcony, looking at the Hawaiian sunset. The sky had changed from golden to beautiful shades of pink, orange, red, and amber. The palm trees swayed in the breeze and the ocean sparkled. The air was fresh and I breathed it all in. Heaven was a place on Earth. I just had to choose to stay there.

And I thought to myself, *The world really is beautiful.*

# Healing Myself

*Making the decision, and doing it alone.*

I left the Waikaloa resort knowing that I had to recover. I wanted to live again, and I wanted to save myself. I just didn't know where to start.

The day after my attempted suicide, I got onto a plane to fly back home with my mother. We met my grandpa at the airport to return my grandmother to him, and when he hugged me, he whispered into my ear, "Get better please, ok?" I couldn't meet his eyes, and his words had done more to trigger me at the time than to urge me on my path to recovery. But I climbed onto the plane with tears welling in my eyes, because my grandpa wanted me to live again, and I wasn't sure if I knew how to anymore. It had been six months of calorie restriction and rapid weight loss, and two years of disordered eating habits. I had lived with an eating disorder for so long that I didn't know what normal meant anymore. The old Julia - the girl both he and I wanted back - was long dead. If even recovering wouldn't bring her back, what would I become? What was I going to do?

On that five hour flight, my life changed forever.

If you ask me what saved my life, I'll either give you the long explanation: personal overcoming of struggles, a good support system, a hell of a lot of strength - or I'll give you the short and simple truth: caramel corn.

I'd picked up my lunch from the airport terminal Starbucks, where I bought an egg white wrap and an overpriced fruit cup. Mental calorie math tallied up the numbers to be 290 for the wrap, 80 for the fruit, but a total of 350 if I didn't eat the melon pieces. I'd wanted to challenge myself to a drink, but at the cash register I balked and opted for a water instead. Just as usual, I'd chosen a safe lunch. *You couldn't break out of old habits even if you tried, Julia* I chided myself as I paid the cashier and grabbed my food.

My mom peered over at my lunch from her plane seat, a look of disappointment in her eyes. After last night's fight that had amounted to a standstill, she had obviously been hoping for change that I clearly was not yet willing to create. So she stared at the food, eventually accepting it and turning away to watch an in-flight movie and eat her own lunch. I ate my food; it tasted good, but I wasn't enjoying it. Every time I looked down at my plate I saw nothing more than a failure. I wanted to get better, I wanted it more than anything. But every time I made a choice, every time I went to eat, I made the wrong choice and I hurt myself once more. My eating disorder came naturally, it was easy, it was reflex. It overpowered me in every way and had been going on so long that I didn't know how to win. I had finally found myself a prisoner in my own house. I wanted to leave. But I couldn't find the keys.

Before I'd left, my therapist had asked me to write my Goodbye Letter. I'd written it on a particularly hard night in Honolulu, scrawled onto a tear-stained sheet of lined paper. I ended up transcribing it onto my laptop and throwing the original paper away when I got home, but on the flight I pulled out the rumpled sheet from my bag and looked out the window. I traced my finger over the messy handwriting, remembering every single word I had written. And then I read it in a hushed whisper out loud, inaudible to anyone but myself over the sound of the roaring jet engines as we sped off the runway into the clear blue sky. I spoke to my eating disorder, telling it everything it had done to hurt me. Telling it that I was done, that I was strong enough now, that I didn't need it anymore. I told my eating disorder that I was leaving it here on Kona, where it could never hurt me. Every word was a lie. I didn't realize that I had been crying until I folded the paper back up, noticing it was fresh with new tears, mixing with the dried up old ones and blurring the text. I placed it back into my bag and looked out the window at the fluffy white clouds dotting the bright blue sky as we climbed in altitude. The island grew smaller and smaller down below, and I watched it knowing fully well that my letter hadn't worked. I hadn't left my eating disorder down there on Hawai'i. It was still there. I couldn't believe that I'd thought, even just for a second, that the letter would seriously cure me. Nothing that therapist had ever told me to do worked anyways.

But those words - those words that had meant something to me when I'd written them down - echoed in my mind, empty in meaning. Nothing more than hollow promises I had made on paper, to appease no one but my therapist. I wasn't doing any of this for myself. The letter, the trip, even eating for the sake of others, so they would see me making "progress" and just leave me alone. I was living for the sake of others. I needed to live again, I needed to recover, but I had to do it for me and me alone. And that meant I needed to nurture, care for, and learn to love a person and a body that I had grown to hate.

This moment was where my life changed forever. I wrote a short essay about it where I go more into detail, and that essay is included in chapter 10. But something in my mind clicked. I made the connection. Psychologists call it insight when you find the answer to a problem you've been struggling with for a while. I call this my miracle. Right there, in the stale atmosphere of an airplane flying 30,000 feet above the sea, my mindset changed from one of defeat to a new hope. On that plane, my destiny - a future that I was so sure would be a slow death - changed with one single moment. This was where I started recovery.

My mom was sitting next to me with a bag of Moose Munch Chocolate-Covered Caramel popcorn, crunching as she watched her in-flight movie. It had been years since I'd last had one of my old favorite snacks, and Moose Munch had long ago been scorned for its butter fat, its sugary caramel, its thick chocolate coating. My mother was shaking the popcorn out of the bag onto a brown paper napkin and picking up pieces one by one, popping them into her mouth with a crunch. After she finished eating what she wanted, she folded up the bag and tucked it into the seat-back compartment for later. I stared down the bag, my eyes flitting to the nutrition label that faced me. Three and a half servings in the bag, each bearing a punch of 300 calories. Just the idea brought my heart rate to a quick beat, and my palms began to sweat. Was I seriously going to do this? I had to.

*I'm doing this for me*, I said to myself as I gingerly reached out and grabbed the bag, unrolling the top. *I'm doing this for me,* I repeated as I fought the urge to shove the bag back into the pocket as my mom stared at me incredulously. *I'm doing this for me.* I reached into the bag, pushing popcorn pieces around with my fingers until I found a little one coated in chocolate. *I'm doing this for me.* I brought the popcorn piece to my lips, biting down and feeling the chocolate coating melt on my tongue, the caramel saccharine and sticky in my mouth. It was the best thing I'd ever tasted. *I'm doing this for me.* I swallowed the piece of popcorn with a gulp, and my shaking hand crept over to the bag, reaching in for another piece.

That was when my mom reached over, gently taking the popcorn bag from my hands. She shook the contents of the bag out onto the napkins, and a tumble of plain caramel and chocolate covered popcorns fell onto the tray table. I watched with my breath hitched as my mother plucked a chocolate covered piece up with her manicured fingernails and reached over to my tray table. Almost tentatively, as if asking for permission with her eyes, she placed the piece of popcorn onto my napkin. I could already feel my eyes clouding with tears as I picked up the piece of popcorn and laid it on my tongue, crunching on it. I couldn't meet her eyes, I was too close to breaking down and crying. She was watching me eat, and I was letting her, and I was letting *myself.* But I glanced up and gave her the smallest smile that I could muster, and granted her permission to feed her daughter.

My mom, meticulous in everything she does, proceeded to sort out every single piece of chocolate covered caramel corn from the bag of Moose Munch. There were significantly less chocolate pieces than caramel pieces, and the pile that she placed onto my little napkin was no more than a small mound probably worth 300-400 calories. I expected her to take the remaining plain caramel pieces and funnel them back into the bag and continue on with her movie; she'd already eaten some caramel corn. But my mother, always the unprecedented woman, did something that I never would have expected. As I slowly pushed myself into eating every last piece of chocolate covered popcorn on my tray table, she ate the caramel pieces alongside me. I kept flashing back to the night before, when we had fought in the hotel room until 9:00, me sobbing on my pull-out couch while she told me how she had been let down. The quiet storm of last night's fight ebbed in my memory as I sat with my mother in a moment that seemed almost tranquil: a weary mother and her dying daughter, sharing a bag of life-saving caloric treats. Together, we finished the bag of Moose Munch, and I collapsed into my seat with caramel sticking to my teeth, my arm draped over my aching stomach as I battled back the feelings assaulting my mind. I couldn't quiet the voices in my head, guilting me, calling me a fatass, a pig, every name under the sun. I was well aware that I had not consumed so much in one sitting in over half a year. But I sat there and I let the tears silently fall, because I had taken the first step towards healing myself, and I had done it with my mother by my side.

I didn't get up during the five hour flight to retreat into the cramped airplane bathroom and shove a finger down my throat. When I landed at LAX, I was greeted by my father and his same sad eyes. All he saw was a daughter who was seemingly even skinnier, at her frailest. I was at rock bottom, but the only way to go was up. As he pulled me into a hug, holding my broken body in his arms, I silently willed a message into his mind: *I'm going to get better now.* In the weeks that would follow, I would watch his happiness return as he saw his daughter getting... not okay, but better than I had been in months. In him, I saw another real reason that I needed to recover. When I gained my life back, I watched the people I loved recovering too. I had been passing along my pain onto them for far too long.

I couldn't stop thinking about the popcorn for the rest of the day, and the thoughts plagued me as dinner approached. Normally, when I had a rare binge like this one, I would re-dedicate myself to an even more restricted meal, a "right" to correct my "wrongs." Had I followed old habits, I would have skipped dinner and gone to bed hungry.

That night I had a big dinner of six cheese ravioli, two strips of veggie bacon, and a bowl of salad for balance. And I finished it off with a cookie.

Coming home with a fresh start changed everything. The house I had grown to feel unsafe and attacked in became a refuge of safety where I could finally begin my real recovery. I hadn't left my eating disorder in Hawaii, of course. I still carried it with me, and on too many days to count it would manifest itself and harm me once again. In my miracle moment, I wasn't casting away my eating disorder forever. I just decided to finally fight it.

Being back in California meant that therapy had to start again. On my first appointment back, I walked into her office, sat down on her too-saggy leather couch, and passed her a printed, double spaced copy of my Goodbye Letter. She pored over it for minutes, reading every word slowly and eventually nodding with satisfaction. I sat for 45 minutes and listened to her rattle off the exact same advice that she had given me in our last four sessions, and probably the same things she said to her other clients. My eyes were almost glazed over by the time the appointment was over, but my mind was racing in a panic - I had so many things I knew that I should be telling her, that I should be opening up about. I was at therapy and I wasn't doing what I was supposed to do: talking. She interrupted her jabbering multiple times and asked me if I wanted to tell her anything or add to the conversation, but I gritted my teeth and repeated, "No, nothing really happened on the trip." I told her nothing about the suicide attempt. I told her nothing about the moment. I didn't even cry. I felt empty as I sat in front of her, listening to her words go in one ear and out the other.

This wasn't working for me.

I firmly believe that therapy can be a valuable tool for both people struggling with mental illness and neurotypical people. It offers the valuable freedom to let go of your problems and just talk to someone, and have them listen. But like eating disorders themselves, people's paths to recovery are unique, and mine didn't happen to involve a therapist. I got my therapy from speaking with my sister, my friend, and you, as I write this book. But when I sat down with a stranger that I couldn't bring myself to connect with, I couldn't tell her the truth and let go of anything. All therapy did was stress me out, and remind me that I was living in a recovery plan built by my parents. I didn't want to recover for my parents. I wanted - I *had* to do this for me. So I decided to dismantle their plan and rebuild it on my own terms. For me, that meant quitting therapy. But that might not be the right thing for everyone, maybe even anyone.

When I told my dad I wanted to stop seeing her, I expected a yelling fight in the car. But almost cheerfully, he said, "Ok. Why? I thought she was helping?" I searched my brain for an explanation that made sense. I couldn't just say that she wasn't helping, because even though she was crappy as therapists go, she had made me write that letter. Or that she was a waste of money, because our insurance plan covered her. I certainly couldn't say the truth: that she had threatened to escalate my diagnosis if I didn't attend more therapy or group sessions, that she scared the hell out of me, that I really never wanted to see her face again. So I just settled on, "I don't know, I'm just not really clicking with any therapists." He accepted it and drove me to Taco Bell, where I faced my fears and had my first quesadilla in four years. It was delicious. I never saw the therapist again.

Being back in California also meant that the weigh-ins needed to start again. Mediocre as my therapist had been, she had permitted me to avoid the scale while in Hawaii as a way to lift stress and focus on getting better. While away, I had checked by myself twice, once on the old, inaccurate mechanical scale in my grandparents' bathroom, and once in the spa of the Waikaloa resort while I was supposed to be getting a facial. There was nothing more terrifying to me than the scale, forcing me to face the numerical value of what I had done. It was even worse that my mother wouldn't let me do it alone - I had to have someone there to corroborate the number, ensure I wasn't lying again. So naturally I chose my sister.

I soon came to realize that the reason I feared the scale so much when I came home was because I knew that I was in the right mindset. I knew that I was finally recovering and that I was going to be okay. But the number on the scale didn't show my healing mind and my new resolve. It only displayed my lowest weight, the near-deadly number that showed nothing more than the fact that I was still iller than ever.

But the recovery plan I had designed for myself on the plane - eating just enough to gain a tiny amount of weight each week without being too overwhelming - was starting to work. Within the first month, I gained two pounds (miniscule when compared to the fact that I had lost nearly 20) and my sister, who held my hand while I stepped on the scale and celebrated with me as I slowly got better. I was clearly making her life harder, something I confirmed when we had a doctor's appointment and we were filling out our questionnaires that the pediatrician makes us complete before our appointment. After checking the obvious boxes like *Have you been sleeping regularly?* and *Have your periods been regular?* there laid the question, *Has anything been causing you stress?* with five blank lines to fill up with writing. I glanced over while she was just finishing up her paper, and I saw her answer.

- College applications
- My sister's eating disorder

I should have realized the effect that watching me tear myself to pieces had on her. She had been there, living with me as I had dropped 20 pounds and brushed with death, and she was living with me as I tried to rebuild myself after it all. I was leaning on her as a crutch, using her as my safe space, and forcing her to be the bridge between the broken relationship of me and our parents. And despite all that, I'd never once paid any regard to how she must have been faring in all of it. I was feeling so much pain, and I never stopped to notice how I was passing some of that along to her as she had to watch her little sister struggle. It was her last year of high school; she clearly didn't need more stress in her life, but still I had never given a second thought to what this was doing to her. I had tied her down and pinned her wings when she needed to be preparing for adulthood and flying high. For that, I will never forgive myself and how selfish I had let myself become.

I started my freshman year of high school, just a little bit healthier after two months of recovering, but still incredibly sick. I was getting better, eating lunch every day at school, and sticking to my plan. Yes, I was gaining the weight back at the slowest possible pace, but my plan was working nonetheless. The full process of my weight restoration, starting in July when I'd returned from Hawaii, took nearly two years. The entirety of this battle was an effort on my part to gain the weight without overwhelming myself. Sometimes it was a half a pound each week, sometimes a quarter, sometimes nothing. Whatever I could muster without falling into relapse or triggering myself into another vicious cycle. It seems counterproductive in theory, but it was the compromise I had found between my mind and my body that would keep me healthiest. Gaining too much too fast would throw me back into a disordered mindset, and I would end up starving again, losing the progress I'd made. Giving too much to my physical health would damage my mental health, and indulging my mind too much would harm my body. There was a happy medium for me, and it came in the form of baby steps. So I took my time, pushing myself as hard as I could without breaking. It was painstaking, frustrating, and I hated every second. But I did the best that I could do, protecting myself along the way in the only way I knew how.

The months and days drifted by. Every two months or so I would have another visit to the doctor's office, sans the normal bells and whistles of blood tests and blood pressure and peeing in a cup. These were eating disorder checkups, where I would come in, step on the doctor's scale, measure my height, and have a chat about my progress with my doctor. Thank God I actually like my doctor, because she made the whole horrid situation that much lighter. She didn't make me feel like the biggest problem in the world, because she dealt with this all the time. It wasn't foreign to her like it was to my family. I was sick, and she was a doctor, there to help me get better. Nothing more to it than that. I admired her no-bull approach to my eating disorder, and with her, I felt more open and comfortable discussing my health that I ever had with my therapist, my nutritionists, even my parents.

As my BMI started to creep back up and I finally got back on the percentile chart (at my worst I had fallen below the bottom 1% of BMI for my height and age group), the eating disorder appointments spaced out, from every two months to every 4, to every 6 months. They didn't stop until August, the month that I started my junior year of high school. But I kept getting better, and every time I went to a checkup and she scheduled the appointment for an even longer interval later, I took it as a new point of motivation. I was getting better, and I could keep going.

Nothing lasts forever, and eventually my sister was leaving for college and I found myself an only child for the first time in my life. I isolated myself even more, something that might have been a negative thing before but allowed me to focus on myself even more. Now that my sister was gone and the weigh-ins were finally over (my mother had stopped demanding them at a certain point), I began to work on my mental health instead of just my physical health. The process of rehabilitating your body is so much easier than healing your mind. Sophomore year held intense emotional struggle and growth that I kept to myself - I had to. My friends at the time never talked about feelings or personal struggles, and we were growing apart by the day. Even my relationship with the girl who I had called my best friend had crumbled away before my eyes, even though I denied it like crazy. I had great teachers and a caring counselor, but I was terrified of crying in front of them. I had no one to talk to at school, and no one to talk to at home. So I did it solo. It was lonely, but I think that I'm stronger for it today.

I weathered the path of recovery, and I did it alone. It started on a plane when I realized that I needed to save my own life for my own sake. It never really ended. I guess if you asked me when my formal period of "recovery" finished, I would say with my final eating disorder checkup in August, but truth be told, I'm still rebuilding everything that I lost today. My body may be healed as much as it can be, but I will never be able to go back to the way I was before my eating disorder. And I don't ever want to. Because despite the immeasurable pain that my eating disorder brought me, it gave me the most glorious gift of strength. I may have fallen, but I learned how to get back up.

Last month, I had the privilege of seeing Celine Dion perform in concert, and she graced my ears with a song that rendered me a shaking, sobbing mess in the back of the balcony. Her song, called "Recovering," was about her journey through grief and rehabilitation after the death of her husband, her true love. But when I Googled it after the concert and pulled up the Youtube clip, I read the comments and saw I hadn't been the only one moved to tears by her lyrics. Sufferers of anxiety, depression, bipolar disorder, and yes, eating disorders were writing to Celine in the comments, telling her how her song motivated them to continue on in their recovery. I can't put the full song here in these pages, but it has managed to perfectly encapsulate my recovery, and apparently so many others', through just a few verses.

*I am recovering*
*The faith of a child*
*By a part of my heart*
*I was reckless and wild*

*I am recovering*
*The hope that I lost*
*The part of my soul*
*That paid the cost*

*Little by little, day by day*
*One step at a time*
*Shake off the devil*
*Take back my peace of mind*

*Well I'm going back to the start.*

# What Not To Say To Someone in Recovery
*Because you'll only make it worse.*

It's a word that's thrown around way too often. *Triggered.* It's used as humor, as jesting, to express a mild annoyance. *Coach is making us practice in the rain today. Bruh, I'm triggered.* To anyone who has ever battled with mental illness, this is the most infuriating thing in the world, the recreational use and trivialization of the word triggered. And yes, I bet someone is reading this and thinking, *Damn, she's getting triggered.*

To someone with a mental illness, a trigger is a situation, thing, even just a word that has the power to destabilize and mess with the mental health of someone if provoked. A comment that seems like a small thing to one person can completely derail the progress and stability of another person without them even realizing it. The hitting of a trigger throws off the coping mechanisms; it overwhelms and consumes until the pressure is too much. They come in all shapes and sizes, from microaggressions to yelling arguments, and they can cause anything from anxiety attacks to suicide. So yeah, triggers are kind of a big deal. Not just the trivial joke they have somehow become in cringe culture.

At my worst, one wrong phrase uttered by a well-meaning family member, or even a fleeting look from my dad could send me into a crying fit, shaking on the food. And now that I'm recovered, some of those old triggers affect me to this day, showing themselves as remnants of a lost time of rampant disorder, crippling insecurity, and a broken mental state. By now I have just accepted them as a boundary I have - a struggle I may never overcome, but nonetheless can live with. They are just another part of me, as they are for other people who have made it through their mental illness or are working to recover from it.

I do my best to manage and avoid the ones I can, and trigger warnings (a written warning that discloses the contents of a potentially traumatic piece of media before it can be viewed) are incredibly important for me when I am on social media. But there are certain things I can't avoid, and they set off flashbacks of the trauma that I've fought so hard to move on from. The most violent trigger of mine I have ever encountered are graphic depictions of suicide in films and television. When I watched Hannah Baker's suicide scene from *13 Reasons Why,* problematic and unrealistic as that series is, I collapsed into a shaking heap on the floor of my bedroom, choking on my own breath as I sobbed for nearly a full hour. I knew it was fake. I knew it was a combination of fake blood and good acting. But when she slit her wrists with a shrieking gasp, strangled cries coming from her throat as she sobbed in the bathtub, I lost it. It was too raw, too *familiar,* and I now knew that I wasn't strong enough to see that ever again. Getting to know my triggers and finding my boundaries as I've moved through recovery has been a process of trial and error, sometimes at the expense of my well being, but it has been valuable for understanding how to keep myself safe.

Of course, these sensitive spots can make it 100 times harder for a loved one to talk to and help someone struggling with a mental illness or in their recovery process. No matter how much you think you know a person, the diversity of triggers make them nearly impossible to pin down and avoid every single potential injury, even if they are your own. A trained psychologist who had been working with eating disorder patients for 20 years managed to hit three of mine within our first appointment, and there's no way she could have known to avoid them. It's impossible for me to outline every single trigger to avoid for every single sufferer, because every eating disorder and every person is unique. A good 75% of my triggers were things that I felt deep, troubling emotions towards but could mean next to nothing to someone else. But there's that 25% of triggers that are universal and absolutely crucial. That's what I'm going to be talking about here.

But the most important thing to remember if you want to help your loved one struggling with an eating disorder or ED recovery is to keep in mind their humanity. Treat them as a *person*, not a basket case. During the time between my intervention and the start of my recovery, I'd withdrawn all hope from getting better and getting help because of how I felt; prodded, poked at, policed. A patient in my own home. No longer a daughter or a sister. Just an immense (ironic because I was *not* immense) problem that no one knew how to solve, or even where to start. My mom always wanted to put me on a scale and monitor my food. My dad just looked at me with the saddest eyes in the world, and in his mind, I saw what he was thinking: "how did I fail her?" When I felt that I'd changed in their eyes from a sick daughter to a defiant deviant, unworthy of redemption, I started to believe it myself. I truly imagined that they saw a delinquent in juvie and not their broken, battered child. Maybe I really wasn't worth saving. After all, I wasn't worth trusting, and everything I did had to be watched.

At one point, a nutritionist even asked me to keep a food journal of everything I ate throughout the day. If you're a survivor, or a doctor, or a nutritionist, or even anyone with common sense, you know that this is the stupidest thing ever. Food journals are how people *keep* their disordered eating habits. Throughout all the nutritionist and psychiatrists and therapists that I visited, they all made me feel the same way: like an unsolvable issue, when I just needed a friend.

What I'm trying to get at here is that you need to treat your struggling loved one with caution and the utmost care, because the wrong thing said at the wrong time can lead to a downward spiral quicker than you could ever imagine. People: they say the darndest things. And most of the time they mean well, but sometimes the right or wrong approach can be the difference between a step towards normalcy and an anxiety attack. A successful meal or a bulimic purge. A deftly handled rough patch and a suicide attempt. The more you know, the safer your loved ones will be.

"Just eat." It's so much easier said than done, but isn't everything? You wouldn't tell someone with autism to just speak, and you wouldn't tell someone with schizophrenia to just calm down. It needs to be recognized that eating disorders are just like other mental illnesses in that you cannot just snap out of it. Of course, the first step to this would be accepting that eating disorders *are* in fact a mental illness, and destroying the misconception that a sufferer isn't eating because they are in control.

"Just eat", my mom would say, handing me a big meal that I couldn't bring myself to touch because I hadn't cooked it, I hadn't counted out the calories, and I couldn't face all of my fears at once. "Just drink it" my dad would say, plunking a bottle of Ensure Plus in front of me while I cried into a pillow. I couldn't put these things in my mouth and chew and swallow like any normal person would. When they put down that food that I knew I couldn't eat in front of me and said, "Just eat," my body was crippled with fear, my stomach tightened, and I squirmed and cried and couldn't bring myself to feed my body. Even if I wanted to. Even if every cell in my body was screaming for something to live off of, my brain was too sick. It wasn't just overwhelming, it was all-consuming. For months on end my eating disorder had trained me to fill my mind with revulsion and disgust at the sight of something I had deemed wrong. What used to be so easy now scared me out of my mind. And the only way I could feel strong, powerful, *in control*... was precisely what was killing me.

Instead of telling me, your loved one, to "just eat," you approach me gently. You sit down, you don't stare at me too much. There's really no way to approach this the right way, because either way I'll probably still freak out. But telling me to "just eat" implies that I'm choosing to not eat. I didn't choose this eating disorder. And at the place that I'm at now, I can't just choose to eat and get better. I have the capacity to get better; every person with an eating disorder has it in them to get better, they just have to be at the right place to accept that capacity. You cannot force it to just happen. Eating this dish may cause you relief, but it causes me self-hatred and rampant guilt, and I might go upstairs, out of sight, and hurt myself even more. So don't tell me to just eat. You have to sit there and let me process this in the best way that I can, and be there with love and support. I'm struggling. Be gentle. Be kind. You can't fix me just like that. But you can be there to catch me when I fall, and be there for the process of it all.

### "Wow, you ate a lot!" Please never *ever* call attention to how much I ate if I had a large meal. It might be a relief for you to see me feeding myself, but I didn't do this for you. It was hard enough to eat, much less to eat in front of you. When you remark on how much I ate, the only thing I hear is that you were watching me.

One of the hardest things for me to deal with during recovery was eating with someone who was having less than me. Throughout the whole meal, I would have an intense pit of guilt in my stomach as I forced myself to eat the larger meal. I knew it was what I needed, it had the calories necessary for me. I knew I had no right to control anyone else. But my brain kept telling me, screaming at me that this was wrong: I had to have the least, I had to be the most "disciplined." I had to hold onto that control. Letting someone else eat with me was hard enough. But I couldn't help but feel their eyes on me, watching, because I was scared that inside their brains, they were tearing me apart and judging me just as harshly as I did to myself.

So if I did happen to eat more than you at a particular meal, don't call me out on it. I felt bad enough coping with the fact that I had a large meal, I don't need you to make fun of me for it, even if you mean well. *Especially* if you are saying "good job" like I'm a dog or a baby that you were tasked with feeding.

Don't put the focus on the food. My mind is always there anyways. Take my mind off of the constant, persistent thoughts of eating and weight and calories that I'm struggling to get away from. Put the focus on life, and help me feel like a person again. Me, your loved one, needs to be loved now more than ever.

## "I wish I had your willpower!"

Believe me, you don't want any piece of this. What's funniest about this comment, besides it being wildly offensive, is the fact that what sufferers of eating disorders lack is the willpower society has painted an eating disorder to be. If I had willpower while struggling with my anorexia, I would have willed myself to "just eat" and live again. I would will myself to keep food down and stop burning out my throat with every bulimic purge. I would will myself into a normal eating pattern and be able to stop the binge eating disorder with ease. But eating disorders have nothing to do with the romanticized image of an iron-clad will, forcing us into starvation and self-hard. My mental illness wields absolute power over me and my actions.

So whatever fleeting diet plans you are trying to stick to, please don't tell me you want my will. The truth remains that nothing about disordered eating or any mental illness is a choice, and an ED is no less or more of a mental illness than schizophrenia,bipolar disorder, and ADHD. My eating disorder is not a manifestation of my vanity and shallow ideals; it feeds off the deep seated insecurities I carry in my schema. It warps my brain chemistry to interfere in simple everyday activities. It tears my life down around me, reaping physical, mental, and emotional harm to me and the people I love. I have no willpower. I wish that I could will myself to live again, to stop killing myself, to be happy. But I am sick, and I never wanted to be.

# "You need to control yourself."

What an ironic and cruel thing to say to someone who has no control over their actions and brain. I cannot tell you how many times I was told to pull myself together and just *get over it,* both by my parents and even an ill-trained therapist. Eating disorders are seen as being hyper-controlling about what or *if* you eat, when it is purely the opposite: lacking control over what or how much you eat, no matter how much you want to live.

It's almost a vicious thing to say to me, your loved one, while I spiral out of control in a body dictated and ruled over by a mind that is not my own. With anorexia, I cannot harness the strength to eat the food in front of me, no matter how much I wish I could be okay. I tell myself that I'll do better eventually, maybe at the next meal or the next day. I never do. With bulimia, purging is my addiction and I wish that I could stop burning my tongue and my throat with acid, even though I know it's so wrong. Every time I do it, I promise that it's the last time. It never is. With binge eating disorder, I have no control over what my body is doing, as my own mind screams abuses at me and implores me to stop, consuming me from the inside out with guilt. I lie on the ground after the binge, willing this to be the last time I do it. It won't be. With schizophrenia, I cannot command the voices in my head to just *shut up,* because those voices aren't my own. With bipolar disorder, I'm not sure which person I'm going to be today, and there's no way that I get to decide. With depression, no matter how many times you tell me to "just be okay," I cannot will myself to happiness. Mental illness in itself is a lack of control.

## "This is hard for me to deal with."

And it's even harder to live with the illness yourself. It's the habit of egocentric human nature to make someone else's struggle all about you. My eating disorder made the lives of my family much more difficult, and I was *constantly* afflicted with guilt over this. I felt horrible enough about the excessive cost of my endless doctor's appointments and supplements that were keeping me alive. I watched as my parents aged before my eyes, seeing our fights and my declining state killing them right along with me.

Put your loved one's safety first. Let them know that you love them unconditionally. I know it's probably hard for you to watch them struggle, but you can't even begin to imagine what they are going through. Be patient and present, but do not make their suffering all about you. An eating disorder is no conscious choice, and there is nothing more selfish and cruel than treating someone else's life-altering struggle as nothing more than an inconvenience. Nothing in this situation is about you, it's about your loved one. You didn't cause the eating disorder, and you can't fix it. But making them feel guilty about what they cannot control to make things easier for you is wicked. However much it hurts you to watch your loved one at war with themselves, never lose sight of the fact that they are in more pain than you could ever fathom.

## "Well, at least you get to gain weight. I have to lose weight!"

I was told this in jest a few days after I started my recovery. I was struggling, vulnerable, and I was told that "getting to gain weight" was a privilege. That I was lucky. I had torn my body to shreds and dropped to my lowest weight, nearly dying twice from starvation and suicide. I now faced a journey ahead of me that would not only consist of restoring almost 30% of my body's weight, but also coping with a broken body image, crippling anxiety and depression, and a destroyed relationship between my body and mind.

There would be nothing glamorous or fun about the next three years of my life spent restoring my physical and mental health. I wasn't living in a state of constant indulgence on pizza and ice cream and effing french fries. Your effort to diet does not in any way compare to medical weight restoration. My fight to recover was hard-won, and brought me more pain and trial than anything else I will ever experience. Yet time and time again, I see the mental illness that nearly killed me and the recovery process that nearly broke me glamorized and trivialized. And for what? A joke to lighten the mood? This needs to stop.

## "You look a lot better!" I'm sure you mean well. But all I hear when you say this to me is, "I've noticed that you've gained weight." Better rings negatively on my ears, and while you might be telling me I look healthier, you're also telling me that you're looking at my body. Something that I spend all day focusing on and trying to hide. You're telling me you notice it as much as I do, and that you're noticed that it happens to be bigger now. I'm abundantly aware of this, so please, don't mention it. Take my mind away from my disorder when we are together unless I want to talk to you about it. I don't need another doctor, I just need a friend.

## "You are being selfish." Fuck you.

# The Aftermath, and How I Picked up the Pieces

*You know what they say... mind, body, and soul.*

As I write this, it has just been a few months since I went to my final eating disorder checkup with my doctor. It has been three and a half years since I hit rock bottom. It has been three years since I made the decision to save my life. It's been two years since the last time I thought about committing suicide. I'm not healed yet. I'll never be healed. But if you asked me how I'm doing today, I would say *I'm doing better*.

Like any battle throughout history, this one that I fought did not come without repercussions. But this one was a civil war. And both sides lost. My mind, and my body, and in more ways than one.

Of course there was the obvious hit that my physical health took. I was dying, and I looked it. Looking back on photos from that time was and still remains painful for me, and whenever I find them, I delete them. I didn't see anything wrong at the time, but now I look back and I'm shocked at how blind I was to the destruction of my own body I thought that I prized so much. I took down over 25 posts from the fashion blog I had wrote at the time. Those pictures are no one's business but my own, and it's nothing that I want impressionable young girls to find on the internet. It's sickening to see how a bad thing that makes its way into your life with good timing reaps nothing but destruction.

August 2015, two months into real recovery.

It took me over a year to fully restore my weight. The process was nothing less than grueling. Ignorant people love to glamorize the medical weight gain process and even eating disorder recovery, saying it must be so fun to pig out on junk food all day, eat whatever you want. French fries and pizza all day. Of course, if that's how you want to restore your weight after an eating disorder, do what you can and must to get yourself to a healthy weight again, because there is no one-path-fits-all on recovery. For me, it was nothing like that, because even when I made the decision to get better, I was still very much stuck in my eating disorder. I still avoided my "fear foods," even if I did introduce a few like potatoes, hummus, vegan butter and vegan cheese. And watching that scale go up slowly? Oh, that was torture.

The number on the scale means nothing more than a relationship between your body and its gravitational pull to earth - it's simple physics, really. It does not measure beauty or self-worth, it does not determine whether you deserve happiness and love. I tell myself that before I step on any scale, although it's something I rarely do today for the sake of my mental health. I whispered to myself during recovery every time I stepped on our cold glass electronic scale in the laundry room, "You are so much more than a number." But every time that number flashed on the little blue screen, and it was higher than the last time, I could feel my heart pound and my breath hitch. Towards the beginning of my weight restoration, I would have weeks where the number I saw on Saturday would determine whether I ate well for the week or reverted into old restrictive habits. I often had to remind myself that I needed to take it one week at a time. Even one day at a time. Nothing is permanent, and that goes for good or bad things. All pain must pass eventually, and I had to believe that there was a better thing in my future. Even if it wasn't in sight yet.

After nearly two years of weight restoration and bi-monthly checkups at my doctor's office (a major source of anxiety as well), my doctor told me that I was at the low end of a healthy weight, and she was fine with me maintaining there. I was overjoyed, and I saw that the fears I had brought into recovery were without any foundation. My body wasn't destroyed like I had anticipated. I'd gained 20 pounds, which seemed like a lot on paper, but I looked pretty damn good.

Initially in recovery the weight you gain seems to go to your stomach, which incidentally was the part of my body I was and still am most self-conscious about. But as time goes on, that weight redistributes itself and you start looking healthier, and normal.

My face was filled back out, my eye sockets were no longer sunken in and dark. My legs could fit back into my jeans again. I had real actual hips again and I could slay a dress. My arms got a little bit of body back so they weren't just bones covered in veins and skin, although they are still the part of my body that carries the least amount of fat- and therefore still look a bit skinny (nothing some weight lifting can't fix). I love my new butt too. And I'm not even remotely embarrassed to declare that, because the fact that I can declare love for a part of my body that I once hated every inch of brings me awe beyond words.

My hair had been dry, brittle, and thin. Every time I brushed my long brown hair, chunks would fall out and I would leave the hairbrush filled with my shattering locks of hair just as starved of nutrients as the rest of my body. I was developing bald spots in the back of my head and had to start gelling my hair strategically to cover them. Recovery made my hair shiny, nourished, and strong again. My nails stopped breaking and peeling away. My bones stopped making cracking noises in the night. My immune system was boosted up again so I wasn't getting sick at the drop of a hat. I no longer needed naps in the midday, because my brain was getting enough calories to function. Watching my body come alive again was fascinating.

But one consequence stayed from my darkest days. During my eating disorder, I lost my menstrual period. This is medically diagnosed as secondary amenorrhea, a common symptom amongst emaciated women. Most cases of severe eating disorders see the reproductive system pause for a few months, usually less than a year. I lost mine for three and a half years.

The typical effects of amenorrhea are irregular periods in the future, hormonal imbalance, and irregular hair growth. I experienced large hormonal imbalances that have caused problems with depression, uterine pain, and chronic migraines as I moved through recovery, and even today I have my fair share of irregular periods (either abnormally long twelve day periods of heavy bleeding or extremely short and acutely painful five hour long nearly-bloodless periods where my abdomen feels like it's being ripped apart). But I had been abusing and damaging my body for far longer than was typical, and the result was a punishment far more severe: infertility.

When my doctor told me this, alone in her office while my dad stood outside, I didn't have a reaction, I just nodded and said okay. This might seem like I'm stone cold or dangerously naive. As of now, I'm pretty sure that I don't even want kids in the first place. And it's not like I have absolutely zero chance - we have no way of testing it, but it is overwhelmingly likely that after such a long period of secondary amenorrhea, this is my reality. I am not devastated by any means about my lack of ability to produce a child, and this could be a callow sentiment that I will come to regret later on in life. I'm not sure how to feel about my infertility, because the thoughts of struggling to get pregnant is something so unrelatable to me right now. But I do know that I would like the *option* to have a child of my own, especially since it's something that my body is designed to do and I can no longer do that. It's frustrating to know that my eating disorder robbed me of an opportunity so important to life - of course, by no means is a woman's sole purpose to birth a baby, and people who say that it is a "woman's duty" can go shove themselves- but for me, infertility symbolizes something that my eating disorder robbed me of, something I can never reclaim from it despite years of recovery. I had the chance to heal almost every other part of my life, but there is one thing that I may never be able to escape. And perhaps it's even harder to grapple with that than it was to recover in the first place.

The mental effects of this period in my life were integral to who I am now. In a way they made me the woman I am today. I'm so much stronger because of these things. Do I wish them on anyone else? Hell no.

Bridging the gap between physical and mental effects of my eating disorder, body image has been one of the longest and most confusing struggles that I've grappled with in the aftermath. Primarily because I spent so much time lying to myself about it.

My body dysmorphia actually got worse the more my recovery progressed, and was something I dealt with during my relapse more so than my primary disorder. Part of that must have something to do with the fact that it's hard to see yourself as fat when you have a BMI of 12, but while my body image was not as debilitatingly bad as that of some other sufferers of eating disorders, my relationship with my body was nowhere near healthy.

A large part of my body image during my eating disorder was based upon denial. You'll hear it in the essays and writing I composed during that period, in chapter nine of this book. Every paragraph I wrote is tinged with the lie I was feeding myself: *What you're going through cannot possibly be a real eating disorder because you are happy with your body.* To that, I can only quote Luke Skywalker and say, "Amazing. Every word that you just said was wrong." Part of why I wanted to include those essays I wrote in this book is because it is extremely compelling to read the account of my eating disorder from the perspective of an unreliable narrator. I was sick, and it shows in my words. And it's interesting to me that while writing those narratives - essays I never intended to share with anyone but myself - I still held back the truth and lied on paper about what I was feeling. Perhaps it was because I had told myself for so long that I loved my body and was killing myself to protect it that I was beginning to truly believe that.

As I moved through recovery, my problems with body dysmorphia became more tangible, more intense. My hatred towards my body during my disorder was shrouded and quiet; during recovery it was bold and unconcealed. As I came back to life, the hollows from bones under skin being filled once again, the perceived insecurities I had battled with manifested themselves before my eyes. The stomach I was constantly covering with my arms was bloated as my digestive system struggled to take on regular amounts of food after being starved for so long. My thighs were filling back in, and I reacted with a sick dismay as I began to feel them touch when I sat down again. It got worse still when I was about 15-20 pounds into my weight restoration, almost fully healed physically but struggling each day mentally.

What if we stopped letting the way we see our bodies run our lives, and we just started living? What if we realized that life is passing by while we delay the action of living until we reach our unattainable goals? *When my waist is 24 inches, I'll be happy. When my thighs don't touch, I'll be happy. When I'm ten pounds lighter, two sizes smaller, when I fit into those jeans, when I fit society's standards of beauty, I'll start living.* And we keep promising ourselves, over and over again, never realizing that life is here. It's happening, and we are wasting both our time and our happiness as we reach for toxic ideals that will never be enough to make us happy.

One day I decided to do something that I'd been avoiding for a almost a year. I decided to look in the mirror. I stripped down until I was wearing only a bralette and underwear, and I forced myself to stand there and stare at myself. For months, I'd avoided looking at my reflection because every single time, I hated what I saw. Sometimes I would even walk into the bathroom with my eyes closed because I needed to pee, but my body image was so terrible that I didn't want to catch a glimpse of myself in the glass at risk of ruining my day. So standing there, half-naked behind my locked bathroom door - no escape - I forced myself to look at what I had become so afraid of: myself. There I stood, and I examined every single part of my body in silence. My calves in my eyes had always been bulky and stubby, but in the reflection of the mirror I just saw lean, normal calves, just like every other girl at school. My thighs were just my thighs - with the slight jiggle that every thigh has. My stomach was only ever flat in the morning, before I started to drink water or eat. It was just my stomach - toned, abs peeking through on the top, but never quite defined enough for my taste. When I turned to the side, it wasn't completely flat, as I'd drunk some water beforehand. And I sat there for what felt like forever, repeating, *And that's okay.* It took me a while to believe it myself. But that session in the mirror, baring my body and soul to everything I had avoided facing, was a step in the right direction.

There were days that I couldn't bear to look at my reflection in the windows of classrooms while I walked down the hall. I knew that what I was seeing in myself was a warped version of what everyone else saw. I was not overweight, I told myself over and over again. It didn't change the fact that there were days that I felt so disgusting that I couldn't wear anything with a waistband, constantly aware of it digging into the skin of my stomach. I was weathering a patch of both bad body image and intense depression when I had my relapse about half a year ago today. A combination of a nasty breakup (not from a boy, but a best friend, meaning that it hurt ten times more) and generalized depression were already on my plate. My sister had been urging me to see a therapist for months, so often that I eventually lied to her and told her that I had scheduled an appointment, conveniently "cancelling" it a few days before so she wouldn't ask questions. For one reason or another my body image was particularly crappy at the time, and I had gained some weight - four miniscule pounds that seem like nothing in theory, but made me feel like a cow.

I didn't plan to start restricting - I just subconsciously *did.* I stopped eating lunch at school one day a week, then two, then all five days. It seems like a small thing, skipping a meal, and I know for a fact that a huge amount of my fellow students do the same thing. But once I started I couldn't stop skipping it - it became an addiction, a game. And with a mind susceptible to addiction, I knew that what I was doing was dangerous. But I couldn't stop. When my stomach growled in fourth period I would ignore it and keep working all the way until the end of the day, because that was all I could do. Eventually I got it back under control, but it showed me that I wasn't quite as recovered as I thought I was.

Depression and body dysmorphia were codependent throughout my recovery, with my struggles with my appearance feeding into the despondency I was already experiencing. It is still something I struggle with all the time. It touches every part of my day, from my hatred of trying on jeans in a dressing room to the way I find myself sitting, legs crossed, arms draped over my midsection, instinctively trying to shrink myself. The difference is, I've learned to stop listening. I no longer let it affect the way I harm myself through restriction, because I know what can happen, and I will never let it happen again.

My journey through depression has ebbed and flowed, hitting deep points both during my eating disorder and throughout the past few years, but its lowest point accompanied the worst few months of my life and intensified the pain I felt during them. From the period between my intervention and my decision on the airplane, I was at rock bottom, living in a body fighting to live in a mind that was fighting to die. It was so painful a time in my life that I can't even remember it all clearly, just a blur of feeling like there was no way out of the hole I'd dug myself into. Who'd have thought you could hit rock bottom at the age of 13? I cried myself to sleep every night. My breakdowns came nearly every day, and I simultaneously felt intense waves of emotion and bleak emptiness, all the while internalizing it and letting it build because I was so ashamed of it all. I'd become something that I couldn't even recognize, and it scared me out of my mind.

Therapy was little to no help. It wasn't just the fact that I couldn't feel comfortable crying in front of myself, much less as stranger, but the way she spoke to me left me feeling like all the responsibility for my situation was on me and me alone. I couldn't put into words what I was feeling, because there was no way to describe it and do the pain justice. Depression is the intangible. It's the empty, sunken feeling you have when you wake up in the morning. It's knowing you have so many things to do and responsibilities to fill but not having the strength to do them. It's not showering for three days, leaving your teeth unbrushed and your hair uncombed, forgetting to take care of yourself.

So with therapy leading me nowhere, I fought off depression alone. And that was the best thing I could have done. As someone who has been fiercely independent all my life and fairly introspective, it was crucial to me that I kept up this independence. It kept me in control of my life and taught me how to keep my eating disorder at bay on my own. Rock bottom became the foundation for me to rebuild my life, and as my will to live and succeed came back, my depression faded into just another part of my life. While it comes back in waves, I no longer let it rule over me, and I've learned how to live side by side with my depression and keep myself safe.

Someone once told me that anxiety is normal. "Everyone gets nervous, right?" It's a typical thing within the life of a teenager, or anyone for that matter. But it's extremely to differentiate between anxiousness as a human emotional state and anxiety as a mental disorder. Anxiousness is the butterflies in your stomach before a test, the sweaty palms when you're out on a first date, the quickened heartbeat and rush of adrenaline you can't help but feel in any nerve-arousing situation. Anxiety is all of that magnified by 100 times; it's feeling crushed under a pressure you can't quite explain and can never alleviate, it's second guessing every decision and every word that leaves your mouth, it's a hypersensitivity to chaos and disarray. It's feeling extremely uncomfortable and trapped in your own skin, it's watching and feeling everything come crashing down you all at once and knowing that you cannot hold everything up with your two hands, it's drowning while you watch everyone around you breathing just fine. And it's incredibly dangerous to normalize that. So please don't tell your child that it's a typical teenage experience to feel trapped in your own body, to stop trusting people they love, and to feel intense, loud, screaming fear at everything and anything. Despite its definition being constantly trivialized and objectified as an adjective for stress, anxiety is a serious problem, and should not be normalized.

At my worst, anxiety attacks would come nearly every day, and every single one was related to food. The worst one that I can remember was triggered by a Wednesday night argument with my mother over my slow progress during recovery. It had started with hyperventilation, which had rendered me speechless as my quick gasping breaths interrupted any chance at talking to my mom. Throughout the attack I was sobbing, black mascara and thick liquified eyeliner running down my face like I was in a soap opera, shuddering heaves spurting from my mouth as I choked on air. I got so upset that my nose started bleeding uncontrollably, the quickly-flowing blood streaming out down my chin and all over my chest and bra. It looked like a murder scene, and lasted for 45 minutes (thankfully the bloody nose lasted for only five of those minutes, because I might have bled out). I locked myself in the bathroom with the rainbow on the wall, staring at the vibrantly painted colors as my breathing slowed down and my parasympathetic nervous system kicked it.

One of my biggest fears was having an attack at school - the ultimate display of my broken mental state. During the worse period of my eating disorder and early recovery, I actually managed to hold it in at school, despite the abundance of triggers I faced on a daily basis. I *did,* however, have to miss a few class periods in the morning on a few occasions because of a particularly bad attack involving my family. This would usually include me crying on the living room floor, my dad yelling at me because he didn't understand why I was crying, and my sister crying while trying to get my dad to calm down and stop yelling. Quite the familial affair.

Eventually, as I recovered, the primary subjects of my anxiety shifted away from eating disorder and broadened its expanse. The first major attack that I had at school was on November 9th, 2016 when I walked into class on the day after Donald Trump's election. Suddenly it was all too much. I had cried myself to sleep about it the previous night, and barely held myself together as I drove to school in the morning, but it all hit me at once that *this* was the reality I would have to live in.  The world as I knew it had changed overnight, and I had not prepared myself for the results I was now facing.  I knew my teachers were going to address it, I knew that I would find no comfort in my friends who were just as shellshocked as I was, and I knew that there were boys walking around my school wearing red hats in victory.

One of the teachers I was closest with that year stopped me as I tried to walk past into class, my head down and my hands shaking as I tried to hide the tears that wouldn't stop flowing.  He talked to me in the hallway as I hiccuped on my words, trying desperately to take in oxygen but choking on each breath.  I was letting the words spill out of mouth at a speed that was probably unintelligible, and I could feel the eyes of 30 students on my through the floor to ceiling windows of the classroom.  They were watching me and talking about me behind the door, and knowing that those unheard words were being said added what felt like ten thousand bricks to the pressure on my chest, threatening to crush me.  And when he finished comforted me and left me in the hallway to calm down while he started the lesson of the day, a fresh round of tears hit me as I realized that this was the first time I had let my peers see me cry.  I was so good at hiding the cracks in my armor, and today it had fallen to pieces, and I'd done nothing to stop it.  I took this as a sign of weakness.

A year later, one of my friends died a sudden and unexpected death.  I found out in French, and had cried quiet tears all period in the back of the classroom, holding myself together from falling apart completely and just screaming.  All I wanted to do was beat on the floor and scream at nothing because it wasn't fair.  Life and death.  Both of them wouldn't hesitate to take everything from me. No matter how hard I worked and how much I cared, I wasn't in control of anything. It scared the crap out of me.

I held myself together for 55 whole minutes. And in Calculus, I shattered.

It wasn't just my friend's death. And it wasn't just the fact that every single person in the class was now looking at me again, saying nothing while I cried into the sleeve of my jumpsuit. For years I had told myself that letting them see me cry was a weakness. I had worked so hard to gain credence as someone of strength and intelligence, someone who handled every obstacle with ease and grace. I had painstakingly crafted a shield that was crumbling to pieces as I was escorted away to the nurse's office, crying like a baby and shaking like a leaf as the worst public anxiety attack I'd ever experienced hit me like a monster truck. I wasn't invincible. I can't handle everything that comes my way. I am emotional, and as hard as that can be, it is beautiful nonetheless.

From that day, I learned to embrace being *not okay*. Struggling with imperfection, emotion, and anxiety are what helped me through my eating disorder. Making mistakes and falling apart has allowed me to build myself back up again, and I've learned not to be afraid of mistakes. And most of all, I've learned to stop being afraid of the anxiety and raw emotion that was born from my eating disorder and has woven its pattern into who I am. Tears are nothing but salt water flowing from my eyes, and crying is not a display of my weakness, but of my strength. My anxiety and depression were something I tried to hide for three years because I was ashamed. But today I know that it is not shameful to struggle, and I am not a failure because I cannot handle everything life throws my way. We shouldn't be afraid to feel our feelings, to fall apart, and to make mistakes. I spent years being afraid of my anxiety, and letting my anxiety make me afraid of everything else. But by allowing myself to feel my feelings, I am able to recognize the messages they send me to make positive change in my life. I live with anxiety. Some days it's worse than others. But most days, it's just another thing I have, and another reminder of what I went through. I'm still here, battle wounds and all.

I was online one day and I saw a question that really made me think. Can you ever recover from your eating disorder, or does it stay with you for the rest of your life? There's no real answer to this. Some people might recover and never exhibit an eating disorder tendency again. That's not me. I don't think I'll ever be fully recovered. And I don't think I'll ever be able to live a life without my eating disorder. But the difference is that I've learned to stop listening to it. I can survive with that voice in my head, making me doubt myself, internally counting the calories and and telling me to put down the cookie and making me look in the mirror every now and then and pinch at the stomach fat that only I seem to see. A wise, beautiful woman once said it best; "I name that voice, I call her Brenda. And I just say, Brenda, shut the f*** up."

I still compulsively peek at the nutrition label when I'm at the grocery store, and my eyes still go straight to calories, fat and serving size. To be honest, letting go of restrictive calorie counting was one of the hardest things to get over. Those numbers became an addiction in my life -

sometimes I wish I could remember math concepts and biology vocab as well as I remember calorie counts and fat grams. Maybe someday they will fade away to a point where I won't be able to look at a food and rattle off the macros in it. "Calorie Asperger's," as *To The Bone* would say. But those numbers have stayed with me, a little souvenir from days past. And yes, more often than not, I still count calories, often for the purposes of ensuring that I am getting enough. Personally, it's what works for me and keeps me from going insane and restricting once more. That small amount of control I keep prevents me from losing myself again. And that's what real recovery is all about: finding a balance in life. That balance is unique to any survivor, but it's one of the hardest things to find. What works for me might be the downfall of someone else, and that was one of the reasons I was so hesitant to write this book. What if someone were to read my story and decide that recovery was a one-size fits all pathway, following mine to a t and ultimately hurting themselves? Am I ready to be an example, a role model, a success story to symbolize a full recovery?

The truth is, full recovery isn't possible. It's likely I will always feel a rush of panic and anxiety when I'm forced into a family dinner, or a nagging feeling of guilt and disgust when I feel full and bloated after a particularly filling meal. The difference is that I don't run upstairs to my bathroom with the rainbow painted on the walls, lock myself in the stall, and ram my fingers down my throat. Instead of reverting back to old habits, I take a few deep breaths. I center my mind, and I tell myself, *You have permission to eat.* Even if I haven't exercised, or I don't feel "hungry enough," or I ate too much yesterday, or I don't know the exact calorie count of my food, or I gained a pound, or I feel like I've done nothing to deserve food. Through this process, I've made myself stronger over the years. Recovery is not dropping every single part of your eating disorder and being "normal" again. It's finding a new normal, taking everything one day at a time, and learning how to respect yourself and your body once more.

# Words From Recovery

*Essays I wrote from the depths of my eating disorder and my progression through recovery.*

### Skinny Girl in a Judgemental World

As I typed out this title on my keyboard, it felt vaguely familiar to me. Have I read this article before? Is that why ideas keep flowing to my head? No, I haven't read this article. Because no one has gone to write it. I have however, read "Big Girl in a Skinny World." It's an inspiring article written by any given philanthropist, one I've read hundreds of times. It tells about a normal woman, navigating her way around a world of hateful, green-juice-sipping, peroxide blonde, size 0 women. Yes, the message inspires me, and I know it's great to be all about that bass. But let's switch it around, shall we?

Yeah, it's pretty clear, I ain't no size 2. I'm not even a size 0. I'm a petite, small waisted size 00 young lady who shops in the kids section more often than she'd like to admit. (Like, that's where pretty much all my clothes come from.) I stay in shape, practice yoga, do light cardio. I keep my muscles lean and ready to take on an active life. I keep my body healthy, I prefer salads over steak, and vegan rice rollers over deep fried twinkies. I'm skinny, yes. I'm also strong.

But with that first word, a stream of stereotypes hit me from all kinds of places. Skinny means the unhealthy, hungry, thin girl. She gossips about everyone, she's abrasive and aggressive. She looks up to models. She only consumes celery and bland health juices. No, that's not me.

The most alarming part is where these opinions come from. They come from people I love, people who aren't close enough to me to even form a judgement, people I don't even know. Everyone. Do you think I feel good about myself when you tell me you don't approve of how I look?

Yes, this world is driven toward an image of the "perfect woman" being a skinny woman. But it seems that even when that's who you are, you are still criticized just as much. You're bombarded with comments about your body, interrogations about your eating habits, terrible accusations of a multitude of issues.

Here's who I am. I don't fit your stereotypes. I gossip, yes, about little things. But everyone does, you'd be lying if you said you don't too. I can be abrasive and aggressive, but I'd like to think that's not what people think of me all the time, and certainly not what defines me. (It's probably because I'm tired!) I DO admire the Victoria's Secret Angels, they're gorgeous. Don't tell me they aren't. I have consumed celery before, big shocker! But I also love sweet potato fries, and mushroom ravioli, and chocolate cereal. I'm skinny. But I'm strong. And I'm healthy. I can be all three of those if I want to be, just like so many others.

Tall or curvy, short or skinny. We're all amazing. And we are all beautiful.

This one I wrote in December after the trip to Las Vegas, before my first doctor's appointment and before my dramatic weight drop. Reading these words over now makes me cringe- the denial is so obvious in my writing. This was how I coped with the snide comments I would hear from family and friends about my body, my food choices, my slowly-dropping weight. This was the first essay I wrote, and the only essay that I shared with other people. I wrote it to justify my actions. To make myself feel like I was on the moral high ground. They say you can be anything you want to be. It didn't matter that in less than half a year, I'd be nearly dead. I said that I didn't have an eating disorder, therefore, I was fine. And I believed it. So I was fine.

## Letter to my Mom

Mom,

I have a hard time expressing how I feel out loud. Words always sound better in my head, and they definitely make more sense there. But somewhere on the way out, they get twisted and turned into something that doesn't convey what I want to express at all. So I thought I'd try and write instead.

I'm sure Olivia talked to you on Sunday about what I told her. I wasn't able to completely express with total accuracy what I was feeling to her either, but it was easier to talk to her. I hope she passed on an accurate transcription of what I told her.

I want, more than anything, to be happy and healthy. Right now, I just desire with all my heart to enjoy this trip like I always would. Hawaii is an escape for me, and I think that even for just 13 days, this will be a good thing for me.

My doctor agreed with me that I should try and enjoy this trip like I would under normal circumstances. Her recommendations were the following: during the duration of this short trip I should not be weighed or measured, I should not exercise, and I should not stress or overthink meals, snacks, and other food, weight, or eating related things.

I know this might not be something you are completely comfortable with, but she highly recommended this method (I researched it and discovered it is called the Minniemaud), for the short duration of the trip. In the meantime, here is my promise to you.

I promise that I will eat good meals and snacks throughout the day. I will do this <u>without</u> arguments or complaint, and without stress, anxiety, or anger. I promise that you won't have to chastise me or tell me to do things differently if you let me do this. I promise that I will make you proud, and I won't be mean, or cold, or rude to you. I will try to be open, loving, compassionate, and considerate. I PROMISE, absolutely. I will follow through and do my part. Let me show you what I can do. Give me the first day of the trip. You won't be disappointed.

I understand that this is a request to which you might be thinking, "What has she done to deserve this?" I don't deserve your full trust. I'm not asking for that. I think this trip could, if we do this, be the best thing for me. If I am able to let go on this trip of my anxiety, stress, and depression, and just feel happy and normal, I will be able to stop thinking about food as fear and start thinking of it as nourishment that my body **needs.** I will be able to help myself heal without a second thought or a voice in my head telling me otherwise, or that I am going to fail.

Please: give me the first day to show you what I can do. I promise that you will be proud of me. I usually never give promises, because I am always scared that I will fail them. But here, I promise.

Please know that I love you. And I love me. I want the best for me. I think this, right now, would be it.

- Julia

forgot that I had written this. It broke my heart into eces, reading this again. This was before my mom took our trip to Hawaii, where I finally began my recovery. Before the trip, I had been on two weight gain shakes a day along with one protein bar. Despite the 640 calories from the shakes and the 190 calories from the protein bar, I was still eating less than 1200 calories a day, and my weight was either falling or staying at its extremely low point. I was dying.

This letter, sweet at genuine as it may seem, was written to manipulate my mother into letting me starve, without her even knowing it. In this letter I promised her good behavior. I promised to fall into line, follow her orders. That was her approach to making me get better- she would give orders and expect me to follow them. So the first step to manipulating my mother- promise to be a good, obedient little soldier.

I didn't fulfill that promise. I skipped breakfast every day, pulled the buns off my veggies burgers, ordered salads and fruit cups and lied and lied and lied. And throughout the whole trip, she didn't lecture me or punish me when I made the wrong choices over and over. She would just look at me with a sadness in her eyes that still makes me cry today when I think about it.

I'm so sorry mom. I can't believe I put you through this.

### The Day

Three miserable months into recovery, something switched off in my brain. It was the last day of my trip in Hawaii, which had been two weeks of hell. Two weeks of uncalled-for comments on my body and social events that I tried my hardest to appear

102

normal at. It was so hard for me to hide the fact that I was fatigued, depressed, and too weak to participate like I always had. My energy would crash in the middle of the day and I would have to take a nap, and I went to sleep earlier than everyone at night.

I was already three months into the recovery process, and honestly, I hadn't made any progress. Not only had the number on the scale stayed relatively the same, but my mind was in the same place as it had been months ago when my family had intervened in my destructive ways. I was instinctively still trying to eat as little as possible, as light as possible. This was my brain talking. My heart wanted to recover. I didn't want to be so sick. But ingrained in my mind was the iron principle that ruined my life, and kept my recovery from becoming reality.

We were at the airport, about to get on the plane. I had already grabbed a lunch from Starbucks since I didn't want plane food: an egg white wrap. 290 calories. And a 100 calorie fruit cup, since I knew my mother wouldn't be okay with just the wrap. She was having a Burger King Whopper with Fries. I picked it up for her while she waited in the terminal. When I grabbed her bag, the smell of those salty, oily, warm fries wafted into my nose, and a tiny part of me wanted some. But most of my mind was thinking, "Ew. Greasy junk." Since that's what my mind was trained and fine-tuned to think. I was honestly at a point where I thought un-clean food was disgusting.

When we got on the plane, I looked out the window as we took off. "Goodbye, ED." I whispered, just as my therapist had told me to say. "I'm leaving you here." It didn't feel like I was leaving anything there. It felt like I was reciting lines. And I sighed, feeling hopeless.

I ate my wrap, slowly, like I always eat everything. That's the way I eat. It takes me half an hour to eat a slice of pizza. The wrap was delicious. Then I grabbed a fork and went to work on my fruit cup. There was one strawberry which I ate. Three purple grapes, which I ate. The rest was a few chunks of honeydew melons and cantaloupe, which I hate, so I didn't eat those. My mom looked over. I was done with my lunch. It was, for the most part, satisfactory to her. So she looked back over to her movie, munching on some caramel corn she'd bought at the airport.

That was when it hit me. I hadn't wanted the fruit cup at all. I had ordered it for her benefit, and ate it for her benefit. I was tired of eating for the benefit of anyone but myself. I was tired of RECOVERING for everyone else's benefit. I wanted, with all my heart, to live again. And I was the only thing keeping me from being happy. It was time to do this for me.

I was finally done screwing around. I was done driving myself into an early grave. I was done stealing away my own future of children, love, success, and happiness. I was done ruining my own life.

I looked down and saw the bag of caramel corn. It was caramel coated popcorn with a few chocolate covered pieces and pecans mixed in. My mom had stopped eating it and folded it up, intending to take it off the plane and save it for another time. I reached for it. She looked at me, then looked down at the popcorn bag in my hands, almost in disbelief. It was SO unlike me. Caloric, sugary, processed, laden with fat, not healthy in the slightest. She was almost as shocked as I was when I picked up the bag of caramel corn and opened it, peering inside.

I dug through the bag until I found a chocolate covered piece, since I didn't want a plain caramel piece and I genuinely hate nuts. I slowly bit into it, tasting the sweet chocolate melting on my tongue. It took me three tiny bites to finish the one piece. I finished it, then reached into the bag for another. The whole time, I was thinking to myself, "Enjoy this. This is an indulgence you need. And you deserve. This is an indulgence that won't wreck your body, or make you fat. But it's a step in the right direction and it's something you can enjoy while you help yourself."

I couldn't find any more chocolate covered pieces, so I set the bag down. My mom picked it back up, and poured out the contents of the bag onto a napkin on her table. There were a few chocolate covered pieces. She looked over at me, then tentatively picked them up and set them on my napkin. Then she started eating the plain caramel pieces.

I almost broke out in tears. We were sharing a bag of caramel corn, me eating the chocolate pieces and her eating the rest. I was eating considerably less than her, since there were much fewer chocolate pieces, but we were still doing this together. It had been so long since I had done this with anyone, much less my mother.

We finished the bag. I couldn't believe that we had eaten so much. But I wasn't crippled with guilt from eating about 400 calories of popcorn, like I usually would feel if I had "cheated" and indulged in something. I rarely ever binged, since my iron-clad willpower rarely allowed a slip up. But when I did "over-eat" (my definition of over-eat was probably having 5 too many popchips), I would feel horrible and rededicate myself to an even stricter next meal. Instead I felt... different. My mother, by sharing a bag of caramel corn with me, showed me that I wasn't alone. After months of feeling lost, hopeless, and terrified, my mind was ready for a recovery from this disease. Maybe, just maybe, I *had* left something behind in Hawaii.

With a twinge of hope in my mind, I pulled out my pink iPod touch, and opened theMyFitnessPal app I had downloaded two months ago. Back then, it had given me a calorie goal of 1700 daily to slowly gain a tiny bit of weight back per week. And then, I had been terrified at the idea of eating 1700 calories per day. Instead I had ignored the calorie goal. I had been getting about 1100 calories a day instead of what they'd recommended.

Maybe it was obvious, but that was when I realized: if I could just push myself to meet the goal each day, maybe I would see real results and recover for the better. I decided that I would try it for a week. Every single day, I would meet the new goal of 1550 (which was the goal prescribed when I changed my activity to sedentary). Non negotiable. I would do it. I would see if it worked. And I would get my life back.

That day was the first day I consumed over 1300 calories in about 8 months. And the week after that, I worked to meet the goal. I realized that it wasn't such an unattainable goal after all. And I was pleasantly surprised. I had gained half a pound, like the app had said I would if I met the goals. I'll admit, when I stepped on the scale and saw that is was a higher number than the week before, my throat clenched up, my heart quickened, I panicked. And then it stopped. And my body? Not ruined like I had thought it would be if I gained weight. My stomach was still flat, my abs still present. I wasn't bulging out of my yoga pants. The truth is, I had never thought I was fat. I had thought, "Hey, I'm skinny. Let's keep it that way." But it had gone too far. And for the longest time I hadn't noticed, since I saw myself every day and didn't notice the gradual change.

I realized, I can do this. I had finally found my comfort zone, and finally found an attainable goal. My mindset was right and I was ready to live again. Finally, recovery didn't seem like a dark hell anymore. It sounded like something I could achieve.

I'm still fighting. It's still a struggle some days. But I am hopeful that I'm on the right path to healing myself.


This essay was written two months after the day I entered my real recovery. It is perhaps my favorite thing that I've ever written. Where the rest of my eating disorder was a blur, I still remember every last detail of that flight, down to the outfit I was wearing, the view out the window when I whispered my goodbye, the taste of that life-saving chocolate popcorn melting on my tongue as my fingers shook uncontrollably. The way my mom looked blurry through the tears in my eyes as she threw the empty caramel corn bag in the flight attendant's trash bin.

This was my little miracle. This was where my life began again. I'll never forget this moment, and when I told my therapist about it, she told me, "You're lucky that it happened. Had you waited any longer, you might not have been able to recover ."

## Goodbye Letter

Dear ED,

We need to break up. This isn't working.

For a while I lived in denial. I didn't think you were bad, I just thought I was being healthier. I thought treating my body like a temple meant relying on you. It's not that you didn't let me eat at all. You did, but you changed me. You just told me what was bad and what was good. You put me on a pedestal and told me I was righteous when I stuck to your rules, and that I was wrong when I strayed.

You gave me a sense of control, and a false sense of health. You made me feel like I was doing something so much better than others. You told me that I was better than everyone else and that if I truly wanted to be that way, I had to keep going. *I* had to be the prettiest. *I* had to be the smartest. *I* had to be the skinniest. I was eating healthy, right? What could go wrong? And it's true, I was eating very healthy foods. But I wasn't eating enough to nourish myself. I couldn't afford to eat like that, and you didn't realize that. Or maybe you did, and you didn't care. You kept hurting me anyways.

You made me obsessive. You made me terrified. You made me suicidal. I was scared that one misstep away from you would lead me in a spiral of self-loathing, or would ruin my flat stomach with my toned abs, or my hard polished discipline, or some other thing that makes me feel very superficial now when I think back on it.

You've done nothing but hurt me. I never wanted you. I always thought I would be too strong to fall into a disorder like you. For a while I didn't want to use that word. DISORDER. It terrified me that I had something like that. I thought eating disorders were for the weak, and I believed that I would never be so petty or undisciplined to fall into one. The truth is that you don't choose to have one. I never wanted any of this to happen, and I never believed that I would have a disorder. But that's what you are. When I was finally able to admit to myself that you were what you were, I felt crushed and weak, and defeated. But acceptance was a step I needed to take.

You don't hurt me because I hate the way I look. Most of the time, I don't. I always wanted to love the way I look. I was scared that if I changed, I wouldn't love the way I looked. So I thought, what is the way to keep a healthy body? Eat healthier. I did that. But I didn't have to overdo it. I would be so much healthier if I'd let myself relax, let myself indulge every now and then, and let myself be free. You are manipulative and controlling.

I am done. I will not let you hurt me anymore. I will not let you linger in my mind. I am kicking you out.

This doesn't mean I won't eat healthy any more. If I want to have a salad, I'll have a salad. But if I want to have ice cream, I'm going to have ice cream. I won't eat for the benefit of you, or my family, or anyone else. I am doing this for me.

There will be hard days. I know I'll cry a lot. But I think I can come out of this stronger. I'm going to stop feeling sorry for myself, or guilty for having you. I'm going to start treating my body like it belongs to someone I love. Because it does.

I have to love myself. I forget that too often. Compassion towards others is so important, but I need to step back and try to take care of myself. I need to remind myself that I am strong. I am beautiful. And I can do this.

So, goodbye. In the end, I won't miss you.

Julia

# Past, Present, and Future

*Finally, I'm telling my story.*

What you've read is a story that I kept hidden for years. A badge of shame that I didn't want anyone to know about, because it was my biggest failure of all. When I started writing this book, it was as a method to cope with the feelings and intricacies I had bottled up and hidden away. This wasn't meant to be published or put out into the world. But here we are. Somewhere along the way of writing this, I changed my mind and realized that it was time to tell my story; if not for myself, for the sheer possibility that someone out there might read my story at their most vulnerable point and find some peace of mind in it. Maybe I could save someone from experiencing what I did. In the very least, I could educate people on how to deal with eating disorders and perhaps start a very important conversation.

I think that it is so important to talk about mental illness. We've come a long way over the past few decades in terms of how we see mental illness- it used to be so taboo in all forms, and eating disorders weren't even regarded as a mental illness; just a construct made from a woman's vanity. Just ten years ago, most people believed that eating disorders were strictly confined to women, and that a man could never fall into the grips of such a vainglorious phenomenon. We glorified eating disorders in the 60's, revering Twiggy as an emaciated role model and the beauty standard of the era. We aspired to eating disorders in the 90's, when "heroin-chic" meant that willowy bodies, translucent skin, and looking like you were near death was considered grungy and cool. In 2017, we have a Netflix series attempting to "construct a narrative" about anorexia with *To the Bone*, but ultimately doing more harm than good, spurring thin-spo all over Tumblr and flaunting a bony Lily Collins as the heroine. We do not have a cure for eating disorders bottled up in a pill ready to sell to the masses.

Girls *and* boys are still dying.

And no one seems to want to do anything about it.

I want to lift the stigma and the shame from talking about eating disorders, and I hope to do that with full transparency. The raw, emotional, real details of my story are in this book. I cried so much while I wrote these chapters and the essays. Page by page, I relived the darkest part of my life. This is a story that I've avoided telling to anyone. My doctor, my parents, and my sister all lived it with me, but know very little. I've only shared some of the details from this with two very close friends. Not even the girl who was my best friend for fourteen years, who I loved at the time with all my soul, knows about my eating disorder. I would tell her everything, but I never told her this, because I was so ashamed, and after a while, I didn't ever want to talk about it because I thought she would never see me the same way, and I didn't want to relive it all. In this book, I'm coming clean.

Funnily enough, writing this book has offered me more healing and growth than my entire process of recovery, and changed me forever. I've realized that the things I've always tried so hard to conceal aren't such bad thing after all. Because once you stop expecting everything to be okay all the time, it doesn't crush you when you have to endure the next hardship. Once you realize that tears are just salty water coming out of your eyes, crying doesn't seem so shameful anymore. My badge of shame isn't so shameful any more, because today I am deciding to own it, take responsibility for it, and share it with you. For years I was so scared of this story, but that's all it is: a story that holds the potential to help others as much as it helped me. I have nothing left to hide, and I never want to hide again.

I can't erase this part of my life. It made me who I am, it's a part of me, and it's never going away. There's a funny thing that I realized while I was sitting alone on the examination bed at one of my final ED checkups, and that was that if I could go back and never have an eating disorder, I wouldn't. This horrible, painful, deadly part of my life, I wouldn't trade it for the world. Because it made me strong.

My eating disorder taught me to appreciate life. It wasn't until I pushed myself to death that I realized on that airplane from Hawaii that I wanted to be alive. My life was pushed to the limit by my diseased brain, and every day, I was given the choice to choose to live or drive myself into an early grave. Despite all the times I chose the latter, I still kept breathing, my heart kept beating, and when I finally realized that I had so much more to do in this world, I had that choice to save myself and just live. I was given that choice again and again until I finally made the right decision. My eating disorder gave me perspective, and showed me how lucky I am. Despite all the times I failed myself and hurt myself, I still was able to live again when I realized that I wanted to.

Others aren't so lucky.

The journey I went through in order to come to terms with myself and my weight helped me realize how important and personal the relationship between me and my body is. This journey helped me realize my core beliefs of feminism, and the right that a woman has to her own autonomy and control over her body. I couldn't imagine a recovery in which I had no choices about what happened to me, with my parents and my doctors wielding complete control. I might have killed myself had that been the case.

Sometimes I cannot help but imagine what would have happened if I had never had that moment on the plane. Or if my parents had never intervened. Or if my suicide attempt had not failed. The thoughts chill me to my bones, but I believe that had my turning point on the plane never occured, I would have kept starving, dropping lower and lower until I was placed in an inpatient hospital. There I would either undergo a grueling forced recovery period at the hands of nurses and doctors, or watch my organs fail one by one as my cardiac muscle catabolizes, my heart slowly struggling to beat and ripping apart tissue with each pulse. Had my parents never intervened, I might have succumbed to the dark, dizzy feeling that I got when I moved too quickly and collapsed. My mother or my sister might have come home to find me unconscious on the floor and I would be rushed to the hospital where doctors would rush to fix the destruction I had reaped upon myself. And if I had kept swallowing the pills and died in that hotel room in Hawaii, my mother would have come back to find my still-warm body. The pain wouldn't have ended, it would have exploded and brought down everyone I loved along with me.

But I chose to live again. I struggled and I fought, I cried and I fell over and over again, but I made it through a journey of growth and self-actualization that is an ongoing path for me today. After every mistake that was made, I still had a second chance, and I will never take that for granted. I feel gratitude for the fact that I am still here today. I am forever thankful for my journey through recovery that allowed me to rebuild myself into the strong woman I am today. And I am grateful that today, I am telling my story. There are two days in the year that you cannot control: yesterday, and tomorrow. I cannot erase my past and undo my eating disorder, but I no longer want to. I don't know where the future will take me, but I now believe that I have the courage to take it on. Today, I break my silence, and I stop being ashamed. I will no longer live in spite of my past, I will live *with it* in harmony. Darkness rises, and light to meet it.

My eating disorder gave me strength that nothing else could. Going through recovery, and doing it on my own, was the hardest thing I've ever done, and will ever do. I've grown into a fiercely independent person, for better or for worse. Going forward into my life I know that I can do anything. I'm a survivor.

# If You're Struggling
*NEDA HOTLINE*
*(1800) 931-2237.*
*NATIONAL SUICIDE PREVENTION HOTLINE 1-800-273-8255*

You're not alone. It may seem like it, but you're never alone. I know it hurts. Whatever point you're at right now, I want you to know that it's not over. It can get better if you're willing to fight for it. Believe me, life is worth it. Staying is worth it.

See, there's a certain fine print to suicide or giving up on living that no one reads. And it's that whatever pain you're feeling, giving up on your life and killing yourself won't end that pain. It just passes it on to someone who loves you. Ending it all doesn't free the dead, it captures and torments the living. Even if you feel like there's no one who loves you, there is. Someone will be affected by the loss of you, because you are a unique, beautiful, wonderful person. You are. They will feel the pain you are feeling right now. So please, don't let them.

If you are struggling, just like I was, please talk to someone. National Eating Disorders Associate, or NEDA, has an anonymous hotline. During recovery, I called in over ten times when I needed someone who understood what I was going through. There is no judgement for what you are struggling with. It's not your fault and it never will be. And you don't have to be alone.

Talk to a therapist, a parent, a friend, a doctor, a teacher, or someone you feel safe with. Please, don't give up. I know that opening up and talking about it is hard, but it's the first step. When I hit rock bottom, I didn't see it at the time, but the silver lining in hitting your worst is that the only way out is up. Giving up is *not* the solution. Please, choose to fight. It's so worth it in the end.

I love you.

Printed in Great Britain
by Amazon